PENGUIN
MY NAME IS

S. Hussain Zaidi is a Mumbai-based journalist, a veteran of investigative, crime and terror reporting. He has worked for the *Asian Age*, *Mumbai Mirror*, *Mid-Day* and *Indian Express*. His previous books include bestsellers such as *Black Friday*, *Dongri to Dubai*, *Mafia Queens of Mumbai* and *Byculla to Bangkok*. *Black Friday* and *Dongri to Dubai* have been adapted into the Bollywood films *Black Friday* and *Shootout at Wadala* respectively. He lives with his family in Mumbai.

Also by the same author

Mafia Queens of Mumbai: Stories of Women from the Ganglands (with Jane Borges)
Dongri to Dubai: Six Decades of the Mumbai Mafia
Headley and I
Byculla to Bangkok

S. HUSSAIN ZAIDI

MY NAME IS ABU SALEM

PENGUIN BOOKS

PENGUIN BOOKS
Published by the Penguin Group
Penguin Books India Pvt. Ltd, 7th Floor, Infinity Tower C, DLF Cyber City,
Gurgaon 122 002, Haryana, India
Penguin Group (USA) Inc., 375 Hudson Street, New York, New York 10014, USA
Penguin Group (Canada), 90 Eglinton Avenue East, Suite 700, Toronto, Ontario,
M4P 2Y3, Canada
Penguin Books Ltd, 80 Strand, London WC2R 0RL, England
Penguin Ireland, 25 St Stephen's Green, Dublin 2, Ireland (a division of
Penguin Books Ltd)
Penguin Group (Australia), 707 Collins Street, Melbourne, Victoria 3008, Australia
Penguin Group (NZ), 67 Apollo Drive, Rosedale, Auckland 0632, New Zealand
Penguin Books (South Africa) (Pty) Ltd, Block D, Rosebank Office Park,
181 Jan Smuts Avenue, Parktown North, Johannesburg 2193, South Africa

Penguin Books Ltd, Registered Offices: 80 Strand, London WC2R 0RL, England

First published by Penguin Books India 2014

Copyright © S. Hussain Zaidi 2014

All rights reserved

10 9 8 7 6 5 4 3 2 1

The views and opinions expressed in this book are the author's own and the facts are as reported by him which have been verified to the extent possible, and the publishers are not in any way liable for the same.

ISBN 9780143423591

For sale in the Indian Subcontinent and Singapore only

Typeset in Sabon by R. Ajith Kumar, New Delhi
Printed at Replika Press Pvt. Ltd, India

This book is sold subject to the condition that it shall not, by way of trade or otherwise, be lent, resold, hired out, or otherwise circulated without the publisher's prior written consent in any form of binding or cover other than that in which it is published and without a similar condition including this condition being imposed on the subsequent purchaser and without limiting the rights under copyright reserved above, no part of this publication may be reproduced, stored in or introduced into a retrieval system, or transmitted in any form or by any means (electronic, mechanical, photocopying, recording or otherwise), without the prior written permission of both the copyright owner and the above-mentioned publisher of this book.

A PENGUIN RANDOM HOUSE COMPANY

For

Vikram the great Chandra,

My mentor, my school of storytelling and writing, my guru, my friend

CONTENTS

Introduction and Acknowledgements   ix

Prologue   1

1. Barrister's Boy   14
2. Salem and Sameera   22
3. The First Brush   27
4. Salem and Sanjay   35
5. The Big D   46
6. Scurrying for Cover   56
7. Despair in Dubai   58
8. First Blood   63
9. Salem's Killing Machines   70
10. Salem Imports Rent-a-Killer   77
11. Taming Bollywood   83
12. Conspiracy in Dubai   90
13. An Execution, a Warning   96

CONTENTS

14.	Extradition Embarrassment	102
15.	The Fallout	109
16.	Duggal's Doll	116
17.	The Don's Darling	122
18.	A Starlet's Rise	128
19.	Salem in South Africa	134
20.	Sameera's *Souten*	141
21.	Salem under Surveillance	150
22.	Caught Out in Lisbon	157
23.	The Lisbon Incarceration	167
24.	Love and Longing in Lisbon	173
25.	The Journey Back	176
26.	The New Jersey Connection	182
27.	Sameera Lashes Out	190
28.	Monica the Turncoat	204
29.	Salem's Sojourn to Sarai Mir	211
30.	Salem's One-Woman Army	217
31.	Surviving Reprisals	225

Epilogue: A Don-in-Waiting   235
A Note on Sources   243

INTRODUCTION AND ACKNOWLEDGEMENTS

My Name Is Abu Salem is the third book in my mafia trilogy, after *Dongri to Dubai* and *Byculla to Bangkok*. Though the actual research took four years, this has been a work-in-progress since 5 August 1997—the day I first spoke to Abu Salem. He was holed up in Dubai then; the very day four of his men were arrested in Bandra for planning an attack on the then reigning movie czar Subhash Ghai. It was also exactly a week before the gruesome murder of music magnate Gulshan Kumar.

It has been over seventeen years since, and I have subsequently met Salem on several occasions. There is a deep-seated mutual dislike between us. He cannot comprehend why I'm not in awe of him and why I don't spare my acerbic pen while writing about him. Members of the mafia often live under the illusion that they are a much-misunderstood lot and that they absolutely do not deserve the firestorm of criticism directed at them. For instance, Salem believes he is very good-looking and that he is a good human being.

For me, Salem is the embodiment of all that is vicious about the mafia—unchecked power and random killings. But even ganglords and dons, despite their sadistic streaks, follow a certain unwritten code. Salem breached all of them. For instance, after killing builder Pradeep Jain, he gloated about it to his victim's widow on the thirteenth day of rituals for her deceased husband. The woman had a nervous breakdown.

In a reporting career spanning nineteen years, I'd come across all kinds of maniacs, but never one to match Salem. Incidentally, he belongs to a respectable family, with highly principled parents.

As a journalist and writer, I'm not supposed to like or dislike my subject. Being objective in writing about such people is akin to a surgeon's code to perform a surgery without allowing his feelings for or against the person to get in the way. In that sense, Salem was a complex, intricate and difficult subject to profile.

However, after over four years of steady research, I realized I would need more time to finish my own

INTRODUCTION AND ACKNOWLEDGEMENTS

investigation as several of Salem's trials were nearing conclusion. But time was a luxury I did not have.

~

I profusely thank my publishers at Penguin and chief editor Chiki Sarkar. Her patience and calm pursuit ensured I finished the book as per my standards of satisfaction. Chiki gave me sufficient latitude and liberty to wrap up the book in the manner that I desired. I would also like to thank my copy editor Shanuj and the cover designer Aashim Raj.

An officer who knows Mumbai's criminals and their global misadventures, former New Delhi police commissioner Neeraj Kumar, came to my rescue repeatedly. Mr Kumar had been the joint director of CBI when Salem was in the United States. It was he who nudged the snooty FBI to go after Salem. He was immensely helpful and remained generous with his time, with no airs about his stature and always keen to help me out. *Shukriya, karam, meherbani*, I am so grateful to have you as my friend, Mr Kumar.

Encounter specialist and Crime Branch cop Pradeep Sharma's resourcefulness and ground-level intelligence gave the book that much-needed boost. Sharma introduced me to the slimiest informants and the most well-connected underworld players hidden in the movie

INTRODUCTION AND ACKNOWLEDGEMENTS

industry. Whenever I hit a dead end in my research, Sharma opened the doors of access to me and ensured that I managed to complete my investigation. My profound gratitude and debt, Janab Sharma Saheb.

Bollywood thrives on a conspiracy of silence. But film-maker Sanjay Gupta, himself a victim of Salem's nefarious designs, magnanimously spent hours describing Salem's vicelike grip on the film world. It was Sanjay's valuable insights that threw light on the plight of the film industry when Abu Salem was calling the shots.

My former colleague Jigna Vora, who was associated with the project since its inception but could not continue because of legal ramifications, displayed exemplary investigative skills and reporting chutzpah in providing information on Salem. Jigna also procured several documents and legal papers for the book. Thank you, Jigna.

After the police and journalists, lawyers were the next big link in helping me finish this project. And the biggest help among them came from a lawyer with tremendous diligence and patience, advocate Saba Kureshi. I met her only a couple of months ago when I was close to winding up the book and she helped me understand the complexities of Salem's extradition and its subsequent cancellation by the Portuguese Supreme Court. Saba patiently and painstakingly explained the

INTRODUCTION AND ACKNOWLEDGEMENTS

legal essentials of the case. I would have been accused of several blunders had it not been for her contribution. Thank you, Saba Kureshi.

The other lawyer who helped me was Sudip Pasbola, who paved the way for my meetings with Salem in the sessions court during lunch breaks.

Three journalism students pitched in with their devotion and diligence. Yesha Kotak, Aakash Jain and Bilal Siddiqui transcribed voluminous documents to make things easier for me. Yesha also translated difficult court papers from Hindi and Marathi into English. These young friends of mine are really industrious, efficient and an extremely hard-working lot. I am so inspired by their selfless service and legwork. Thank you, Yesha, Aakash and Bilal, it's unimaginable to work without the three of you.

While writing this book I deliberately decided to avoid seeking help from any journalist friends. However, I had to break this vow to seek guidance from Sheela Rawal. Sheela is editor of investigations at Star News and one of the most intrepid investigative journalists in the country. She is the only one who managed to trace Sameera Jumani, Salem's wife, in the US and to speak to her for six hours. Since this feat could not have been replicated, I sought Sheela's help in using the interview and other background details on Sameera. Sheela quite generously and unhesitatingly helped me with

INTRODUCTION AND ACKNOWLEDGEMENTS

information, a rare trait among Indian journalists. My in-depth thanks, Sheela.

My thanks will not be complete until I mention friends and contacts who gave me their valuable time during my research, legwork and investigation in Dubai. The Gulf capital is still an underworld hub where gangsters spend their lives behind a thin veneer of respectability but have not entirely recanted from their murky past. They were quite helpful and open while talking about Salem. The man who knew him best and feels most betrayed is Malik. He gave me deep insights into Salem's character. Others spoke to me only when they swore me to confidentiality.

My protégé and pupil Rayyan Rizvi, who quit journalism when I did and relocated to Dubai, deserves special mention. Rayyan helped with the research in Dubai. For an entire week, he kept aside all his work commitments to become my driver, guide, researcher, interviewer and man Friday. I love you, Rayyan. You are fantabulous.

Prince Reza Iqbal Mirza of Angoori Bagh, Lucknow, a descendant of the royal family in Lucknow, now settled in Dubai, was enterprising and magnanimous with his contribution to the book. Prince Reza was my 2 a.m. friend and travelled with me to little-known nooks and crannies of Dubai. The prince put his entire office staff at my disposal for admin and paperwork,

INTRODUCTION AND ACKNOWLEDGEMENTS

also lending me his senior assistants for transcriptions.

Zahoor Haider Mirza was meticulous in preparing notes and diligent in the transcription of several interviews that I conducted with various Salem aides in Dubai. Despite his hermit-like regimen of sleeping at 9 p.m. every day, the man graciously burnt the midnight oil for me, poring over his laptop in the wee hours with bleary eyes. Zahoor's accurate and timely notes were of great help.

Zia Rizvi and his wife, Fahmida, of Sharjah also helped immensely in my quest to get the facts right. Thank you, Zia Bhai and Fahmida Aapa.

Lastly, I have to mention that this book would not have been completed without Karan Pradhan, my young colleague since my days in the *Asian Age*. Karan was associated with this book since the first word was written, and devoted several days and nights to ensure that this turned out to be an engrossing read. He was superb as a researcher, analyst and compiler of facts. Had it not been for him, this story could not have been told in the form and narrative as it is in your hands. Karan was indefatigable while converting the book into several formats, from first-person to third-person and then through other narrative styles as the story unfolded.

My sincere thanks also goes out to Kavitha Iyer, my former colleague from the *Indian Express*, who despite her prior commitments browsed through the final draft for any errors and gave her blunt advice about each chapter. It was her fine editing that has enhanced the reading pleasure of the book.

Supreme and most profound gratitude is reserved for my readers. On second thoughts, I can never thank you enough, my readers, who motivated me during the darkest hours to keep writing even when I felt fatigued, demoralized and down. It was your inspiration and appreciation that kept me on my toes. I am humbled by your encouragement.

PROLOGUE

'I can tell you the complete story of Abu Salem as no one else can. He has been my brother and partner in crime since childhood,' said the baritone voice reluctantly over the phone.

My months of research on Abu Salem had hit a dead end. Despite poring through numerous documents and tracking every available shred of information on Mumbai's meanest mobster, I was no closer to unravelling the mystery of the man himself. I needed someone close to him.

The man on the phone said I had to come to see him in Dubai if I wanted to meet him. Dubai, during Christmas? In my desperation, I might have been willing to undertake a mission to Mars. But I was not sure if it was wise or even safe to meet a stranger alone and in a foreign country.

The Central Bureau of Investigation (CBI) and the Mumbai Police had given me huge dossiers of information on Salem, but nothing could beat the knowledge of a man who had grown up with Salem from the time he was barely old enough to walk, leave alone wield a gun. It was too much to resist. And so I boarded my Emirates flight to Dubai.

Salem's life is a study in paradox. He was unique among the Mumbai mafiosi in a number of ways. Born in the village of Azamgarh in Uttar Pradesh, Salem single-handedly rose to become the nemesis of Bollywood bosses and construction czars. No other don's name instilled as much fear in the hearts of the film fraternity as his. He did not merely terrorize film personalities; he extorted from them, had some of them killed, and along the way also helped some strugglers become superstars. You could call him the don of Bollywood.

A middle-school dropout, Salem managed his smuggling business with remarkable acumen, and made millions. A street ruffian, he also had the heart of a Casanova and was married numerous times, including a whirlwind romance and marriage with a film actress. The man who came to Mumbai with barely Rs 100, now had over Rs 5000 crore worth of property in and around Mumbai. The man who used to ogle at photographs of film heroines in his village had been able to sleep with some of the loveliest ladies in the industry.

Working in a world where taking revenge was a part of the job description, Salem never once spoke or plotted against his old boss Anis Ibrahim even after he bitterly parted ways with the D-Company. What's more, despite being such a fearsome terror, Salem was also a soft-spoken and well-mannered man. It was this tapestry of contrasts that pulled me towards his story.

The glitzy emirate of Dubai may be known as home to the world's tallest building (Burj Khalifa), tallest hotel (JW Marriott Marquis) and the largest man-made island (Palm Jumeirah), but for me it is most famous (or infamous) for being a safe haven for the Mumbai mafia. In the early eighties, Dubai was the easiest foreign place for Indians to access. Anyone could get there in two and a half hours, with a visa on arrival for Rs 5000. Whenever the Mumbai Police turned the heat on the gangsters, they would run off to the Arab capital. For less than Rs 20,000 which included airfare and visa, they could shun the Mumbai jails and blend in with the many South Asians who worked in the emirate. To make matters more convenient, Dubai had no extradition treaty with the Indian government during this time; so once a criminal reached this haven, he was safe from the Indian government. The trend that was started by Dawood and his men in the early eighties continued till the late nineties.

Many of the accused in the 1993 Mumbai serial blasts and other major crimes continue to live there and even own several properties in the island capital. Despite Dawood Ibrahim's relocation to Pakistan, Abu Salem's extradition to India and Chhota Rajan's vanishing act, the city still stinks of mafia connections and hideouts. Iqbal Mirchi's Imperial Suites and Sharad Shetty's Ramee Guestline hotels are doing well. Both Mirchi and Shetty were Dawood's confidants when they were alive.

As I landed in Dubai, I realized it was one of the worst seasons to visit. The UAE government was planning the world's biggest pyrotechnics display which would shatter the previous record by over 400,000 fireworks. Tourists were flocking to the country in droves. In an unrelated development, my Christmas meeting had been shifted to New Year's Eve. Just my luck. The whole city went berserk on 31 December.

The venue for the dinner was to be Al Ibrahimi, a Pakistani restaurant near Deira Market metro station. Al Ibrahimi's buffet was regarded as one of the best in Dubai. Delicious tandoori fish, the juiciest nuggets of chicken marinated in yogurt and garlic, a mutton rogan josh that was par excellence, several other Pakistani delicacies and the divine dessert of Umm-e Ali were just some of the treats on offer at the buffet. As I waited, alluring aromas wafting around, I received a call and was asked to come instead to Jumeirah Beach.

I protested that the traffic was chock-a-block and that it would be impossible for me to get there but the man insisted. He was afraid he might be spotted, so he could not afford to be anywhere near Al Ibrahimi.

Following a brief drive through the gridlocked streets, my driver gave up his efforts to drive towards Jumeirah. 'The Dubai government wants to break the record held by Kuwait's fireworks display last year,' he said in exasperation. The sheer scale of Dubai's fireworks display was staggering—it was an incredible show of extravagance and opulence. In six minutes, over half a million fireworks would explode, fizz, twinkle and scream across Dubai's skies.

Hosted by various five-star hotels on the Palm Jumeirah as well as by downtown Dubai's famous Burj Al-Arab hotel and the Burj Khalifa, the midnight fireworks extravaganza was to be split into two parts. First, an intense six-minute display across the Palm Jumeirah and at the 2717-foot Burj Khalifa hoped to seal the world record. This was to be followed by a fifteen-minute display along a one-kilometre stretch of Jumeirah Beach. The present record holder—Kuwait—let off an astonishing 77,282 fireworks over the course of an hour in 2012.

The driver parked my rented car on the side of the road and I began to walk towards the Jumeirah. It seemed quite an arduous task due to numerous security cordons, traffic and the multitude of people. As I began walking I got a call again and was informed of the new venue for our meeting. I was to wait on the highway just across the street from the Burj Khalifa and he would meet me there.

I turned back and re-entered the car and we headed for the highway. The crowd here was relatively thinner and less frenzied but the celebrations were just as splendid. Why had he chosen such a day and time to meet me and tell the story of Salem? I was beginning to feel tired, sleepy and frustrated.

As I waited at the rendezvous point, I felt a tap on my shoulder. I turned to see a nondescript man of medium build, balding and well dressed. On the highway, where the only thing I could see in the dark sky was fireworks, he was sporting sunglasses to hide his face. He did not want me to see his face or look into his eyes.

'Salaam alaikum, my name is Malik, and I am a childhood friend of Salem's. I am not meeting you because I wanted to but I was asked to and could not refuse,' he said curtly. I sat down with my diary and pen, and assured him that all I needed was a couple of hours of his time. But the man was still hesitant. He looked at the sky, sparkling sporadically with fireworks, and asked, 'Do you know that I am a part of the team that organized this show?'

It was this cover that facilitated his trip to Dubai and

his ability to move around incognito. 'We have used over hundred computers to synchronize and choreograph the whole spectacle,' he boasted. Over two hundred expert technicians from the US-based Fireworks by Grucci had been called in to work on the show. The UAE government had spent over $6 million on this record-breaking display.

'Make me a promise,' he said somewhat dramatically, 'no one should ever know that I have spoken to you and told you this story.' 'I promise,' I said and asked, 'but then tell me why Dubai? Particularly at this time of the year.' He grinned. 'I can escape under the cover of the fireworks and disappear. No one will ever know that we met here.' I nodded.

Malik began Salem's story. I began writing furiously on my notepad and later hammering away at my laptop. Malik was a chain-smoker and he spoke through a constant plume of greyish-blue smoke swirling around us. Time flew by and I barely noticed that he had been speaking for hours.

It was close to daybreak and Malik had begun rambling about Salem's links to various politicians. The final salvo of the fireworks formed an artificial 'sunrise' along the seafront, heralding a new dawn for this city of big dreams and unrelenting ambition. Thousands of amethysts lit up the night sky as red and silver fireworks cascaded down the 828-metre tower.

This year's top highlight, however, was the firework display shaped like the petals of the *Hymenocallis* desert flower—on which the Burj Khalifa's design is based. The petals created the illusion of it enveloping the tower. The huge edifice being enveloped in flower petals was a breathtaking illusion.

Atlantis the Palm, at the far end of the Palm Jumeirah, had organized Sandance, its hugely popular monthly festival, on Nasimi Beach, with a New Year's Eve line-up that included DJs Paul Oakenfold and Pete Tong. At the other end, the Jumeirah Zabeel Saray on the west crescent of the Palm Jumeirah, used as a set in Tom Cruise's fourth outing as Ethan Hunt in *Mission Impossible: Ghost Protocol* and often hosts Hollywood A-listers when they visit the Middle East, had a plush party of its own.

It was in this segment of Dubai that Salem owned his properties. Malik said Salem had five bungalows at Jumeirah Beach. He lived in one, used another as an office, while the other three were rented out. 'This should give you an indication of his affluence,' Malik said. The whole story related by Malik was a dazzling account of Salem's rise and growth in Mumbai's underworld, his connections in Bollywood and politics. By this time, the muezzin had begun to sound the azan.

Malik looked at me and said, 'There is only one man who could tell you a better story than this one.'

I looked at him curiously.

'Salem himself,' he said.

After bidding me farewell, he said, 'Khuda haafiz', and left in his car, leaving me alone on the highway. I realized my story would remain incomplete until I met Salem. But Salem was not a free man any more. He was now lodged in the high-security confines of the Taloja Central Prison.

Taloja, a small, sleepy township about fifty kilometres from the tumult of Mumbai, had shot to fame for its exceptionally delicious biryani. Over time, however, the famed Taloja biryani lost its flavour and its cuisine became a matter of history. In the post-Babri Masjid demolition riots, the government decided that a company of the Rapid Action Force (RAF), a paramilitary unit, should be stationed close to the city to respond to any riot-like situation. And that's how Taloja next came under the spotlight. Over the last couple of years, however, this sleepy township shot into the headlines once again when Mumbai's most notorious undertrial, Abu Salem, was shifted from the Mumbai Central Prison, popularly known as Arthur Road Jail, to Taloja Central Prison.

Taloja Jail seemed quite at odds with its surroundings. The jail was surrounded on three sides by the fancy neighbourhood of Kharghar. I wondered how the builders would sell flats in these high-rises. Would they market their flats as Jail View, Main Gate of Jail View, Prisoner's Compound View, etc.? The Bombay High Court had recently clamped down on the construction blitz, issuing instructions that there should be no new buildings less than 500 metres from the jail.

The prison also seemed to have been deliberately built at the foot of the hills in order to provide for additional security. This security is external—to ensure no one escapes. But what if an inmate wanted to kill a fellow inmate inside the jail? How could internal security be fortified? Last year, Salem had narrowly survived an attempt on his life when gangster Devendra Jagtap had fired on him in the jail barracks.

At the massive wrought iron gate, when a burly policeman asked me the purpose of my visit, I told him I wanted to meet Salem. He looked me up and down. My black trousers and starched white shirt gave the impression that I might have been Salem's lawyer. So he just waved me inside without frisking me.

Once inside the jail, it was a walk of another 200 metres to the meeting room. I saw the children of detenues playing in the compound. Infants when their fathers were arrested, they had grown up to be schoolgoing children, studying in class five and so on. Further ahead, I saw an old man whose white hair and white beard were dyed with henna to a shiny red. The man was the 'tiffin-delivery chacha', whose job it was to provide food to several inmates who were permitted home-cooked food by the court.

I then decided to walk to the meeting room, and asked to meet Salem. The meeting room had ten stalls, each with its own glass partition. As in the movies, the undertrials sit inside and their lawyers or relatives sit outside and speak to each other over an intercom. I wondered whether I should pretend to be a lawyer or a relative of Salem's to ensure my smooth passage into the meeting room.

My thoughts were thrown into disarray by a lawyer in the room. He had realized that I was not with any of the bonafide groups of visitors to the jail and sympathetically suggested that I should not push my luck any further. It would be wiser of me, he said, to try and meet Salem in the sessions court, where he is a daily visitor for hearings in his case.

Meeting Salem on the fourth floor of the new building of the City, Civil and Sessions Court outside courtroom number 54 was easier than expected. It was lunchtime at the courts and their recess generally lasts from 2 to 2.45 p.m. I saw him standing in a corner in the corridor, surrounded by his jail escorts.

Dressed in a well-ironed pair of trousers and a checked half-sleeve shirt, he was voraciously gobbling down his lunch of butter chicken and naan, which had been brought for him by one of his lackeys. This would not be the first time I was meeting Salem. He knew of me. He also knew of my previous work and had expressed his disapproval at my portrayal of his love story in *Mafia Queens of Mumbai*. He expected an apology. I offered none.

I reminded him that I was in the process of writing a book about him. He asked quizzically, 'Why a book? Write a movie script on me. I don't like small-scale things like books. Who reads them anyway? I want to do things on a grand scale.'

'Well, I am a journalist and a writer; I can write. I can't write a script or make a movie,' I tried to explain.

'I will help you to make the movie. It will be a mega-budget movie. My story is so interesting that people will see it without getting up from their seats to take a break for a smoke or to go to the loo,' he persisted.

'I can't take your help in any venture. I want to do things in my limited capacity. And with that in mind, I wanted you to tell me your story.' I dug my heels in, expecting a long argument.

But he surprised me: 'I have written some 100 pages of my life story. I am prepared to give it to you if you seek the court's permission.'

Apparently, Salem had given this spiral-bound book to several people to develop a movie script. Meanwhile, Salem's security ensemble had begun to get impatient. They realized I was neither a lawyer, nor a relative, not even a henchman of Salem's. So I had no right to be talking to him for so long.

I left the courts empty-handed that day, but it only took a couple of weeks for me to acquire Salem's handwritten autobiography. While Salem was lodged in Arthur Road Jail, this mini-autobiography had been written by one of his English-speaking cellmates to whom he dictated. Throughout this 12,000-word story, Salem had portrayed himself as a do-gooder, a generous friend, a guardian angel and a messiah for the meek and downtrodden. He saw himself as a hero who had been wronged, but stood against injustice and showed exemplary courage and bravery. What an interpretation of a life full of crime and violence!

ONE

BARRISTER'S BOY

IT HAS TO BE ONE OF the bigger ironies of our times that two of India's most feared criminals were born into the homes of agents of law and order. While Dawood Ibrahim's father was a constable, Salem's father was a noted criminal lawyer in the legal circles of Azamgarh. Nevertheless, his family led a hand-to-mouth existence.

Advocate Abdul Qayyum Ansari, who lived in Sarai Mir, practised in the Azamgarh court. He travelled fifteen kilometres from his home to the court by Rajdoot motorcycle every day. People looked up to him in the semi-urban, dusty sprawl of the town. After all, a motorcycle was one of the signs of a stable and well-to-do home.

Abdul Qayyum and his wife Jannatunissa had four

sons. Abu Hakim was the eldest, then Abu Salem, followed by two more sons, Abu Lais, alias Ejaz, and Abu Jaish. The youngest child was a girl who was named Anjum. It is striking that all the boys had the prefix 'Abu' in their names—this is primarily an Arab Muslim custom. The first name is usually something like 'Mohammad', followed by an epithet like 'Abu Hakim', which means the father of Hakim. It is generally considered polite to call people by this epithet in their name, rather than their first name.

The family owned a flour mill near their home, a major source of income. They used to sell ice cream and ice as well. But when Salem was only five years old, his father met with an accident on the way to the Azamgarh court. His motorcycle suffered a nasty collision with a bus and he was left on the side of the road, bleeding for hours. When he was finally taken to hospital, Qayyum was declared dead.

The Ansari community that Qayyum belonged to is not generally considered to be very well educated. But the lawyer and his brother were exceptions, and had studied as far as college. Salem and his brothers fit the stereotype a lot better, since they all studied up to only class six or seven in an Urdu-medium school before quitting. Salem himself got only as far as Class 6.

What he lacked in education, though, he more than made up in manners. Salem's mother was very strict and though she could teach him very little mathematics or science, she was very particular about etiquette and instilled in him a sense of social propriety. As a result, Salem was very well mannered and highly respectful of his elders. He never cursed or quarrelled; instead, he always smiled and spoke with deference.

After Qayyum's death, Salem's mom took to making and selling beedis in order to earn a living. Eventually, Salem began to show an interest in automobile and motorcycle repairing. By the age of fifteen, he had become proficient enough to be known across Sarai Mir as an excellent mechanic. It was then that ambition—an integral part of Salem's psyche—kicked in. He thought it was time to move to a bigger city where his talent would be recognized. He wanted to eventually open his own car-and-motorcycle repair garage. So at fifteen, he dropped everything, packed his meagre belongings and set off for Delhi. He spent a couple of years struggling in Delhi, repairing motorcycles; but slowly came to terms with the fact that he was getting nowhere.

Two years later, Salem realized the time had come to move on. He didn't know what he would do but he knew he couldn't go back home. The idea of going back to Azamgarh would be admitting failure. So, despite his brothers Abu Hakim and Abu Lais calling him back home to start a business there, he refused. Instead he moved to Mumbai.

His cousin Akhtar Ansari had told him that he owned a shop in Jogeshwari's Arasa Shopping Centre where he sold belts, perfumes and other assorted items. Akhtar's shop was a tiny stall among hundreds of others packed in closely, many of them selling similar items. Naturally, competition was cut-throat and stall owners would try various things to gain a small advantage, including hiring members of the underworld for protection. This would be Salem's first brush with the mafia.

Arasa Shopping Centre had several shops which were owned by gangsters. This was a legitimate front for their illegal activities. So it was usual for the shopkeepers and owners to wine and dine together. Impressionable and unlettered Muslim youths, like Salem, tended to look up to such gang managers, wanting to emulate them.

Salem worked at the shop for three years and over the course of this time became familiar with a man there called Sayyed Liyaqat, who was also known as Sayyed Topi because of his habit of wearing a topi. Sayyed Topi was Anis Ibrahim's—Dawood Ibrahim's brother—point man in Arasa. He handled Anis's extortion activities between Bandra and Borivali, and had been handling such affairs since 1985.

Dawood, Mumbai's numero uno don during this period, had two of his brothers in his gang—Anis Ibrahim and Noorul Haq, alias Noora. Anis played the more important role and, as Dawood's power grew through the seventies and eighties, his brother Anis too began spreading his tentacles in smuggling and land-grabbing across the city. In 1986, Dawood and his brothers, including Anis, relocated to the safe environs of Dubai. Before leaving Mumbai, Anis had appointed several point men, working for him in various parts of Mumbai, one of whom was Sayyed Topi.

Salem looked up to Topi and desperately wanted to work for him. Unfortunately, Topi did not open up to him. He sensed that Salem was an ambitious man and with time might topple him. Undeterred, Salem would keep trying to curry favour with him.

One day, Aziz Bilakhia—known rather cruelly in the underworld as Aziz Tingu on account of his diminutive stature—came to Arasa to meet Topi. Over the course of this visit, he met Akhtar and subsequently, Salem. Aziz and Salem hit it off and became firm friends. It wasn't long before this friendship bore fruit and Salem was introduced to Baba Moosa Chauhan and Riyaz Siddiqui, two other D-Company associates. It was in this way that Salem's circle of contacts began growing and started including many men who worked for Anis.

Salem soon become a diligent soldier. His work for the don included money laundering, collection of extortion money, delivering confidential information and occasionally roughing up people. Anis found Salem to be a reliable lieutenant. Dawood too had heard of him and was quite pleased with his work.

As his stature began to grow slowly in the underworld, Salem began recruiting people. He got fifteen to twenty boys who were willing to assault people, break bones, and smash furniture at his command. He was now also talking regularly to Anis, through Aziz, and conferring with his men in Mumbai.

Soon, Salem began to feel like he was stagnating at the stall in Arasa Shopping Centre. In 1987, he decided to kick up operations a notch and, along with Siddiqui, Baba Moosa Chauhan and Aziz, opened an office in Hasnabad Lane near Gulmohar Road, Santa Cruz, by the name of Lutfi Enterprises. This was supposed to be a manpower recruitment and export office to send Indians to Saudi Arabia and other Middle Eastern countries for jobs—*lutfi*, in Arabic, means gracious, an apt name for the business. Lutfi was also the first office—but certainly not the last—where Salem would hang a huge portrait of Anis on the wall. It's unclear whether this was a sign of his sycophancy or dedication to the man.

For Salem, Lutfi would also be a front for smuggling—with men used as carriers for sneaking in gold and other contrabands. After kicking off his new business of recruitment, Salem started to make frequent trips to Bangkok, Singapore and Malaysia. Unlike other gold smugglers who remained confined to their cities waiting for their contraband to reach the city's shores, he became a globetrotter and frequent traveller. It was a strategy that was to pay off.

When Dr Manmohan Singh took over as the finance minister in the P.V. Narasimha Rao government, the biggest step he took was the liberalization of the Indian economy and the easing of the Gold Control Act. This had boosted the foreign exchange reserves of India and broken the back of gold smuggling in Mumbai. But criminals have always managed to circumvent the law for their own benefit. They refer to it as '*qaede ka fayeda*' (the benefit of law).

The forefathers who had written the rules of smuggling—the likes of Haji Mastan, Sukur Bakhiya and Yusuf Patel—made huge earnings from gold smuggling during the decades of the 1970s and 1980s. But after the liberalization of gold imports in 1992, duty was slashed and non-resident Indians (NRIs) were allowed to bring in five kilograms of gold as part of their baggage by paying a duty of Rs 220 per ten grams.

Never one to give up, Salem began to grease the palms of customs officers. It was an age-old method employed by Dawood. A conniving and corrupt customs officer could be of major assistance in the smuggling of gold. Salem began tapping NRIs who were working abroad and/or had NRI status due to having completed the stipulated tenure of living 180 days abroad.

He began using them as carriers of his gold consignments. The NRIs were allowed to carry double the permissible quantity and would only have to declare half the gold they brought with them. They were charged Rs 22,000 for every kilogram of gold. Sometimes, NRIs travelled back home with their entire family and brought in even five kilograms of gold. Since their wives and children too were travelling, they got the benefit of doubt. And so, the smugglers' syndicate made a sizeable killing on gold smuggling through the legal channel. Salem had set up this kind of network for gold smuggling in all the tourist destinations that were nearest to India. These included Thailand, Malaysia, Singapore and the Gulf countries.

By 1989, Salem had become one of Anis's top lieutenants in Mumbai. The smuggling business also proved to be lucrative, and his boss was happy. People had begun to know of Salem and some had also begun to fear his name and his growing clout. Salem was beginning to enjoy the power and the dread that he evoked. By now, he had invited several of his struggling cousins from his village to join him in Mumbai and become his henchmen. Soon, Salem was being hailed as a hero of sorts in Azamgarh. The villagers began mentioning his name with deference. From Salem, he was now called Salem Bhai.

TWO

SALEM AND SAMEERA

SALEM WAS A WOMANIZER AND A Casanova. He craved female company and could not be without a woman for long. His friends often referred to him as a sexual predator.

Soon after his arrival in Mumbai, he learnt the ways of the city and the finer nuances of chasing girls. Already known to be a charmer, he further honed those skills when he realized that girls were drawn to sweet-talking men. Salem had learnt from the movies that Mumbai's girls are rather stylish and attractive. Ultimately, he wanted to be married to a Mumbai girl so beautiful that she could even pass off for a silver screen heroine. He had seen plenty of movies and knew that a self-respecting hero must have a girlfriend. In his mind, he was as good-looking as any Bollywood hero, so why shouldn't he have an attractive girlfriend?

Barely twenty then, Salem found it difficult to focus on his work and was often distracted. His cousin Akhtar and other relatives scolded him and urged him to get some direction in life, but Salem did not give up his quest for a girl. After he finished his work at Arasa Shopping Centre, he would often go to Juhu beach and ogle at the women there.

Finally, his relatives convinced his mother Jannatunissa to summon him to the village and get him married as he was at risk of going astray in the big bad city. When Salem reached his village, the news of his impending marriage came like a bombshell. There was no way he wanted to get married so early in life, but his elders prevailed upon him and he had to give in.

Salem was wedded to a girl from the village of Khudakpur, six kilometres from his own village of Sarai Mir. The nuptial ceremony was a small affair and only a few guests had been invited. Salem reluctantly brought his new bride to Mumbai and returned to his routine. The marriage was doomed from the start—since the couple was inherently incompatible, and fought frequently—and did not last long. After consulting his elders, Salem took his wife back to his village and sought a divorce. In later years, he would refuse to acknowledge that he had ever married anyone from his village.

However, Abu Kalam claimed that Salem was briefly married before he started chasing girls in Mumbai.

Salem had rented a new flat in D.N. Nagar, Andheri, and he happened to notice a young girl living just across his flat. Her name was Sameera Jumani and she was studying in the junior-level science stream of Bhavan's College, Andheri. Salem was immediately smitten by Sameera's drop-dead good looks and began following her to college every day. Soon, Sameera too, like many other gullible young girls, was drawn to his sharp features and began to fall for him. There was an age gap of five years between the two, but Sameera would not let that dissuade her. She believed that Salem was her man.

Salem would go to her college astride a motorcycle and woo her. Later, when he had a car, he regularly drove around Andheri with the good-looking young woman by his side. 'Salem was aware of Sameera's young age and her devoted love for him. As a gesture of love, Salem would sometimes sing a song from the hit Bollywood film *Ek Duje Ke Liye*, starring Kamal Haasan and Rati Agnihotri. "*Solah baras ki baali umar ko salaam, aye pyaar teri pehli nazar ko salaam*" (Salutations to the tender age of sixteen and salutations to the first glance I ever had of you, my love), he would croon,' recalls one of Salem's close associates.

Her father was a businessman and as soon as he realized that his daughter was interested in Salem, he put his foot down. Sameera belonged to a conservative Ismaili Khoja family and she was forbidden from marrying outside her *jamat*. Salem, too, was a devout Muslim who refused to join the Ismaili faith which was what her family would have required of him.

Sameera's parents were also completely opposed to her having this relationship while she was still in college and they tried to reason with Salem's relatives, but he was beyond reason. They then tried to persuade Sameera to stop seeing Salem, but she was madly in love. She refused to even look at the economic inequality between her family and Salem.

In the two years of their courtship, Salem had grown from a mere shopkeeper in Andheri to a budding smuggler, while Sameera had managed to finish her junior college and gained admission to an undergraduate programme. Then one day, Sameera's parents decided that enough was enough and planned to get her engaged to a suitor from the Ismaili community. Salem then decided to elope with her.

In the meantime, Kalam, the only one amongst the inner circle who knew Salem since he was a child, repeatedly tried to convince him that Sameera was a young girl and he shouldn't ruin her life—not to mention the fact that they belonged to different sects. But Salem had made up his mind and they got married after a courtship of two years, on 4 January 1991. At the time, Sameera was seventeen years old and a minor according to Indian law.

The Jumani family lodged an FIR against Salem at the D.N. Nagar police station and he was charged with abduction. But Sameera threatened suicide and it was only after Salem's family intervened that the Jumanis relented and withdrew the case. Salem was freed and they both relocated to a new house.

Within a few months of their marriage, Sameera learnt of Salem's illegal activities and his underworld liaisons. She was shocked. But there was no going back. She was already married to Salem and he was deeply entrenched in his business. He could neither have been expected to abandon his business which had just begun to give him the comfortable life he so craved for, nor could Sameera have left him as she was far too comfortable in his company.

But March 1993, which changed many destinies in Mumbai, including that of Salem's, was not far away.

THREE

THE FIRST BRUSH

ABU KALAM, SALEM'S CHILDHOOD FRIEND AND cousin, had never seen the inside of a cell. Yet there he was, stripped down to his underwear, his hands tied to the wall and a car tyre around his waist. Aside from his anguished screams, the only thing he could hear was the resounding thwack of the thick police-issue belts as they were whipped across his back.

Through eyes that had long glazed over with pain, he could see four burly policemen taking turns at thrashing him, oblivious to his screams and pleas for mercy. After they'd had enough of beating him with sticks, they began kicking him in the kneecaps, the back, his buttocks and shoulders. One policeman took particular pleasure in slapping him across the face. Kalam, like

Salem, was slightly vain. He believed he was extremely good-looking and this reflected in his style of dressing. It did not take the policeman very long to realize this, so he dedicated himself to slapping Kalam's face till it was swollen or until a tooth chipped. This torture continued for a whole day.

On the second day, Kalam was convinced that the pain would be a little easier to handle, but these policemen were veterans. The longer Kalam continued to stonewall on Salem's location, the worse the thrashings got. But he did not allow the pain to overcome his loyalty and, confident that Salem would send someone to bail him out, Kalam kept quiet. It was at the end of the second day of beatings that Kalam began to get angry at Salem. Every time he was slapped, whipped, kicked or punched, the policemen would ask, *'Salem kidhar hai?'* And every time Kalam would reply, *'Nahin maloom, saheb.'* His loyalty to Salem was unwavering.

Now, after two days of continuous beatings and very little food, water or sleep, Kalam was on the verge of total breakdown. On the third day, he came to the conclusion that Salem had probably made full use of the forty-eight hours that Kalam had bought him, to lie low at some safe location. There was absolutely no reason to protect him any more. Kalam was furious at Salem, and at himself. He began thinking back on the events of the day which had landed him in jail.

One fateful evening, Salem had announced to Kalam that they were going to meet a businessman in Bandra and that he would be handing over a few lakh rupees. There was no explanation provided and none was required by Kalam. Perhaps Salem had some business with the businessman, thought Kalam to himself, and that this was a payment. They set off on a motorcycle and rode to Turner Road. After arriving at the location, Salem began to look around suspiciously. He told his trusty sidekick to dismount and go and meet the man. Salem would join them shortly. Not suspecting a thing, Kalam hopped off the bike and strolled over into the businessman's office.

'Salem and his friend are here,' he announced, 'tell your boss!'

Kalam was taken into the man's office and he swaggered in as if he owned the place. He sat down and cockily said that Salem had sent him to collect the money. The businessman nodded, stood up slowly and walked out of his office. Kalam waited, leaning back into the soft cushion of the office chair, expecting the man to return with a bag of money. Would it be in a black briefcase, he wondered. Before he could know the answer to this question, he was being slapped in the face and dragged by two hefty men in plain clothes to a jeep waiting below the building. Kalam had walked right into a trap.

Salem had probably suspected something fishy and that's why had decided to let Kalam get nabbed rather than risk his own capture. 'He must be around, I don't know,' was Kalam's response to the police when he was nabbed. He wasn't lying—he truly had no clue. The cops brought him to Bandra police station and over the last few days had tried their best to get him to speak.

After three days of beatings, Kalam's face was swollen, his teeth were broken, his eyes were black, and his body was covered with welts and bruises. Enough was enough, he decided. If a policeman were to lay as much as a hand on him again, he would send them straight to Salem's doorstep. Soon, a policeman walked over. Kalam braced for impact.

To his surprise, the khaki-clad man began to untie the ropes that bound his ankles and wrists. He was then made to put his clothes back on. Something had clearly happened, he figured, as he stumbled gingerly. It was only when he saw the lawyer and Salem's friend Riyaz Siddiqui sitting with the police that the penny dropped. After three days of twiddling his thumbs, Salem had finally come through. Kalam was released and Siddiqui led him out to a taxi. The journey was silent. Kalam wanted to save all his words for Salem, and Siddiqui wasn't in too chatty a mood either.

When they arrived at Salem's place, he looked totally remorseless. In his naïveté, Kalam had expected more from Salem. A lot more. The least he could've done, thought Kalam, was hug him for his loyalty and refusal to snitch on Salem. A bit of concern or sympathy about his injuries would have been appreciated too. And while Kalam wasn't looking for any material reward, he would have gratefully accepted one. But Salem was totally indifferent to the last three days of trauma his long-time friend had faced.

That's when Kalam lost his control. He attacked Salem with a barrage of expletives demanding to know why he didn't come to his rescue. After all, they were friends, they had come to Mumbai together and now they were in business together.

Finally, Salem broke his silence. He said calmly, '*Arre, Kalam bhai, yeh toh dhanda hi aisa hain*. Don't take these things so seriously. They happen all the time.'

Kalam simply could not understand how Salem could be so callous and be unmoved by his plight. But he also realized that there was nothing he could do. Salem wouldn't change. The priority was always his own safety and well-being. Nothing and no one else mattered.

But Salem soon felt the tentacles closing in around his own neck in the hands of one of the most ferocious officers of the Mumbai Police. In the late eighties and early nineties, Mumbai was going through a watershed moment when the mafia was trying to establish itself. Gang wars between Dawood Ibrahim and Arun

Gawli, a millworker-turned-ganglord and ex-crony of Dawood, were starting to take their toll on the city. In the meantime, Khalistani terrorists were moving from Punjab to Mumbai (into predominantly Sikh areas such as Bhandup, Mulund and Sion). The Sikhs there used to store weapons, give refuge to militants on the run and plot terrorist attacks. Mumbai's streets ran red with blood.

It was to tackle this situation that the Mumbai Police instituted its anti-terrorist squad (ATS). This was led by an officer called Aftab Ahmed Khan, seen on the silver screen in the 2007 film *Shootout at Lokhandwala*. The ATS office was in Bandra, but its jurisdiction was all of Mumbai city. This is especially astounding when you realize that it was a unit of just twenty-two men handling an entire city's rising graph of violence. While Khan was involved in several violent skirmishes with Khalistani terrorists in Bhandup and Mulund, he was also keeping a keen eye on the increasing clout of the underworld in the suburbs.

He had heard about Aziz, Chauhan and Salem, who were operating between Mahim and Andheri. He sent them a message, inviting them to meet with him. Aziz and Chauhan promptly did so and assured him that they would steer clear of all illegal activity. Salem did not feel the need to meet this policeman. This irritated Khan. How could this hoodlum have the audacity not to turn up when summoned? Khan wanted to teach the upstart a lesson.

Khan was returning to his headquarters one day, in a bad mood after a faulty tip-off, when he and his men happened to spot Salem outside the Arasa Shopping Centre with some of his cohorts. Salem was the perfect target to vent his frustration on. Khan ordered his men to pick Salem up right there and then. The policemen rushed out of their vehicle and set upon him with hockey sticks. The ATS in those days was bereft of any smart weapons, so they had to make do with such unorthodox options. They grabbed Salem and beat the living daylights out of him at the gate of the shopping centre. This would be Salem's first introduction to the ways of the Mumbai Police.

Following the brutal beating, Khan wanted to make an example out of Salem, and instructed his men to tie him by the wrists to the back of the jeep, so that he appeared to be almost crucified across the back of the vehicle. And then, with this novel car 'ornament', Khan told his men to drive to the nearby D.N. Nagar police station. People watched, as a bruised and battered Salem was taken to the police station where he was promptly handed over to the officers in charge.

He was then detained for two days and given a thick slice of the Mumbai Police's own brand of special treatment. While Salem was behind bars and on the receiving end of brutal thrashings, his friend Topi was ambushed and killed by Inspector Emmanuel Amolik near the Yellowgate police station. Suddenly, the position of Anis Ibrahim's top man in Mumbai had opened up.

Somehow, Salem's friends were able to put together Rs 25,000 (a huge amount in 1991) and arranged to have him released on bail. He quietly walked out of the police station with Aziz and Chauhan, who led him into a car. As he returned to the Arasa Shopping Centre to be reunited with his cousin Akhtar, Salem was surprised at the welcome he received. The garlands and applause made it seem like some sort of a hero had returned home from war. Aside from being seen as a hero, the other benefit of putting up with the police's brutality was that Anis had taken notice. He was now talking directly to Salem, who had leapfrogged over Aziz and Chauhan.

As for the ATS, after the 1993 riots, Khan reportedly became too big for his boots and a law unto himself, leading to the squad being unceremoniously disbanded.

FOUR

SALEM AND SANJAY

STANDING ON ONE LEG, THE OTHER knee bent in a sort of bastardized version of the *vrikshasana*, Sanjay Dutt looks positively Godzilla-esque in the promotional material and posters of the film. He stands between the comparatively smaller images of co-stars Madhuri Dixit and Jackie Shroff, the film's title emblazoned below—*Khalnayak*, The Villain.

His clothes are an eyesore—a semi-chequerboard, semi-striped suit ensemble, complete with a white polka-dotted black tie and matching hat. He is tipping his hat jauntily, with a black-gloved hand. But the most bone-chilling part of the look is the demented grin on Sanjay's face—the expression in his eyes screams out pure, unadulterated, evil insanity.

As he says in the movie, *'Jee haan, main hoon khalnayak!'*

Ghai released his film on 6 August 1993, four months after Sanjay was arrested under the stringent Terrorist and Disruptive Activities (Prevention) Act, or TADA. It was a rather unremarkable film that might have tanked completely had it not been for director Subhash Ghai's masterstroke in releasing it when lead actor Sanjay Dutt was in jail. It raked bountiful returns at the box office. To cinemagoers, film and real life had fused. Sanjay was truly the embodiment of his memorable proclamation—a khalnayak.

Born to superstar parents, actors Sunil and Nargis Dutt, on 29 July 1959, Sanjay was always given the very best that life had to offer. The youngest of three siblings (after sisters Priya and Namrata), Sanjay received most of his education at Lawrence School, Sanawar, in Himachal Pradesh. He is believed to have been troubled as a youth and later fell upon difficult times, turning to habitual substance abuse during his teens.

Expectations for Sanjay to join Bollywood were especially high after both his sisters decided not to enter the world of cinema. While Sanjay made his official Bollywood debut in the 1981 tale of vengeance, *Rocky*, his first appearance on the silver screen was actually as a junior actor with a cameo in the 1971 film *Reshma Aur Shera*. Gradually, more film offers began rolling in and through the 1980s, Sanjay began to establish himself as a reliable action hero. With his chiselled physique and regal mane, cinemagoers began to realize that it wasn't his surname alone that was bringing him success.

Big-banner films like *Vidhaata*, *Taaqatwar*, *Hathyar* and a host of others established him as a bona fide star, even as the walls were closing in all around him in his personal life. As his drug problem escalated, the actor was forced into a rehabilitation facility, where he met actress Richa Sharma. Unlike the star Sanjay had become, Richa was a relative newbie in Bollywood with only a couple of films under her belt—having made her debut with the 1985 film *Naujawan*, where she was touted as Dev Anand's find. The duo hit it off almost immediately and were married in 1987. Two years later they had a daughter, Trishala.

Meanwhile, Sanjay's films were doing brisk business at the box office and had transformed him into a cult phenomenon, a trend witnessed most prominently after his 1990 film *Thanedaar*. Starring Jeetendra, Madhuri Dixit, Jaya Prada and Sanjay, the film is another tale of vengeance—a rather common theme in his films—and redemption. It captured the imagination of millions.

Those were the pre-digital poster days and Bollywood poster art was all the rage among youngsters and film lovers. One of the most popular of these prints, sold at railway stations, footpaths and even in gift stores, was a still from *Thanedaar*. It depicted a moustachioed Sanjay Dutt in police uniform, with a carelessly unbuttoned khaki shirt and a police hat thrown on casually. While the man's unmistakable and inimitable machismo was still a major part of his image, there was now a new sense of irreverence and a strong anti-establishment vibe.

Having 'cleaned up his act' and kicked his drug habit (at least as it seemed at the time), Sanjay's life at this point took a new turn and he began cultivating fresh interests and hobbies—premium whisky and fast vehicles (all of which bear the registration number 4545), particularly motorcycles. But his most interesting new pursuit was the acquisition of firearms. He was an avid game hunter and would reportedly never leave home without a loaded pistol in the glove compartment of his car.

On one occasion, Sanjay was even stopped at London's Heathrow Airport for carrying a firearm, even though it was a licensed weapon. Clearly, the troubled son of a respected member of Parliament and his late actress wife, a devoted humanitarian herself, was blurring the lines between his real and reel lives. His action-hero image was beginning to catch up with him and he seemed to have felt a constant urge that could only be charitably labelled as 'infantile', to live up to that image.

The years 1991 and 1992 proved to be extremely

fruitful for Sanjay. It saw the release of the Feroz Khan-directed *Yalgaar*, which became a personal favourite of Abu Salem's. It was, in fact, director Feroz Khan who had ushered Sanjay to the underworld, having first introduced Anis bhai to Sanjay as a good friend. Soon after, Anis bhai had hosted Sanjay at his home in Dubai during the shooting of the film. It was during the course of the shooting of *Yalgaar* in Dubai that Sanjay was introduced to Dawood, Qayyum and others. And Anis had promised Sanjay that if he needed any help in Mumbai, he should never hesitate to call them.

As 1992 drew to a close, the simmering communal fervour in the country came to the boil as a BJP-led mob demolished the 465-year-old Babri Masjid in Ayodhya, Uttar Pradesh. Mumbai witnessed some of the bloodiest riots in the country. The senior Dutt organized help and medical aid for those injured, regardless of their religion, origin or constituency, while the junior too pitched in.

But not everyone, it soon became clear, approved of this Hindu family helping out Muslim victims of the communal clashes. Incensed groups of radical Hindus—including members of the Shiv Sena—subjected the family to abuse, threats and attacks. The otherwise revered MP was actually attacked on a number of occasions, including one instance when an angry mob launched a furious assault on his car. Undeterred, he continued to do his humanitarian work.

His son, however, had just about enough of the threats and attacks. Realizing that the police would not offer special protection even after revolting phone calls (in which one caller allegedly threatened to rape Sanjay's sisters, kill his father and burn down the house), he decided to take matters into his own hands. After all, he rationalized, what good did it do being simply a celluloid hero? After years of playing characters in countless films about redemption and justice, the time had come to be a real hero, and stand up to protect his family.

Enter Hanif Kadawala and Samir Hingora. Disillusioned with the Mumbai Police's inaction, Sanjay shared his predicament with this film producer duo. All he wanted was a means to protect himself and his family. That would entail beefing up his threadbare arsenal of firearms. Having already been introduced to Anis Ibrahim and been a guest at the gangster's home in Dubai, Sanjay knew who to get in touch with for the arms. Eventually, it was decided that Salem would accompany Kadawala and Hingora to Sanjay's residence with an array of guns and grenades.

Reports of the streets of Mumbai being painted crimson in the aftermath of the Babri demolition had upset Salem greatly. The way he understood it, the blood being spilled was Muslim blood alone. His grief for the plight of his fellow Muslims later gave way to resentment against Hindus and, finally, an all-encompassing thirst for retribution. This was in stark contrast to things back at Salem's hometown, Azamgarh. The difference, he believed, was that not a single drop of Muslim blood could have been spilled there, because in Azamgarh, no one dared mess with the Muslims.

Following the riots, Salem decided to lie low. For a few weeks, he stayed out of any sort of trouble and kept his name out of the headlines. Then one day, he received a phone call from Anis, asking how he was holding up. Anis went on to drop a bombshell. Salem would have to make a very special delivery. His job was to hand over some *samaan* to a friend in Bandra (in underworld parlance, 'samaan' usually refers to 'ammunition'). This sounded simple enough, for Salem had run several such errands in the past. But his jaw hit the floor when Anis named the consignee—Sanjay Dutt.

This was the most interesting piece of news Salem had heard in a long time. The young Salem was in awe of Sanjay Dutt and regarded him as something of a role model. In the days leading up to the drop, Anis provided all the logistical information and details. The plan entailed first picking up the samaan in Bhiwandi, hauling it across the city to Bandra and handing it over. The package would have to be delivered directly to Sanjay, in person, at his Pali Hill residence, Ajanta. It all seemed simple enough.

Aziz and Salem set off from Mahim in a white Maruti

car driven by a Gujarati boy, whose name the gangster does not recall. In his CBI confession, he said he was so caught up in the excitement of meeting his hero that he did not pay attention to the car's registration details or the name of its owner. They just didn't seem like important details at the time.

About two and a half hours later, they reached a place near Bhiwandi and waited outside a small hotel by the road. Aziz and the Gujarati kid entered the hotel and made an entry in the register. Money exchanged hands. Shortly, all three of them found themselves relaxing in one of the rooms in the hotel waiting for further instructions. After around two hours of speculation and idle chit-chat, they were all set to make a move.

The trio climbed into a Maruti Omni van that was waiting for them; the goods had been loaded into a specially hollowed out cavity in the boot. This was usually used to store contraband like silver; Salem, in his confession, said he naturally assumed that something similar was to be delivered. In Bandra, they were met by film producers Hanif Kadawala and Samir Hingora of Magnum Video fame, and Baba Moosa Chauhan.

At one point, Samir and Hanif got out of the van to make a call from a cell phone. Salem would later find out that Samir and Hanif had just incurred a whopping Rs 1300 charge on the call they had made to Anis in Dubai. The news was disappointing—the meeting with the Bollywood superstar had been postponed by a whole day.

The next day they headed to Pali Naka and arrived at the Dutt residence. Sanjay greeted the party at the gate. Samir, Hanif and Baba got out and exchanged pleasantries with Sanjay. Nervously, Salem wiped his clammy palm dry on his trouser leg and approached Sanjay, who strode over and drew Salem into a warm embrace. Salem was speechless at the star's affectionate and humble greeting.

There was a uniformed policeman standing guard at Sanjay's gate and the star asked him to leave his post and return in a brief while. Sanjay then asked to see the goods. The cavity in the boot was prised open and his consignment was taken out and laid out for him to see. In his CBI confession, Salem said he was genuinely shocked to see that the samaan consisted of a selection of around nine or ten assault rifles, including AK-56 guns, and between eighty and ninety hand grenades. Salem, whose criminal work at this stage didn't go beyond roughing up victims using a small gang, had only ever seen sophisticated weapons like these in films.

Sanjay examined the weapons and seemed completely at home with the guns. He did not want to keep all the weapons and chose three AK-56 rifles and a few grenades. On the way out, Sanjay hugged Salem again and thanked him for coming. It made Salem even happier when he asked him to come back in a couple of days.

By their next meeting, Sanjay had had plenty of time to get used to the weapons and he explained that he did not want to keep that many weapons at home. He added that one AK-56 would be more than sufficient and then sent Salem on his way with another warm hug. Having received three hugs from Sanjay Dutt, Salem could not stop boasting to his friends and associates for days.

Subsequently, he took the bags containing the remaining weapons to the home of a woman called Zaibunissa Qazi. After the 1993 blasts, the police was leaving no stone unturned in its efforts to put people behind bars. Hanif and Samir had been detained by the Crime Branch and Baba Chauhan had also been arrested. Sanjay's name cropped up in the investigations and he was slapped with charges under TADA.

From a hero, Sanjay had gone to being branded a 'terrorist' in the short space of three months. During a raid, in addition to the AK-56, the police had found five other firearms stashed away in his home. The star's reputation was ripped to shreds and even his father's squeaky clean image was tainted. The man who encashed on the negative publicity of Sanjay Dutt and laughed his way to the bank was, of course, Subhash Ghai.

While all those involved in delivering the weapons

and grenades to Sanjay Dutt's house were booked under TADA, including the star himself, and suffered the ignominy of jail, Salem managed to escape the long arm of the law.

FIVE

THE BIG D

AN ORDINARY MAN FROM AN ORDINARY family in an ordinary locality with neighbours just as ordinary—that was Dawood Ibrahim Kaskar. But what he did with his commonplace roots is what made him an extraordinary leader of the Mumbai underworld. Legend has it that at his peak, the merest mention of his name was enough to make brave men tremble, the very aura that drew Salem to him. Like hundreds of misguided Muslim youngsters in Mumbai, Salem saw the kingpin of the D-gang as a role model. For them, Dawood was a man who rose despite the odds, defied a heavily biased system and emerged successful. Salem was in awe of the man.

The Ratnagiri-born Dawood was among twelve children of Ibrahim Hasan Kaskar, a police head constable in the Mumbai Crime Branch. Dawood spent most of his childhood in the company of street kids, and made his foray into the world of organized crime by doing odd jobs to earn a bit of money for his large family. It was here that he ran into the local gangs. Over time, he crossed paths with the lynchpins of the smuggling industry—Haji Mastan and Karim Lala—and began his own low-level smuggling business with his brother Sabir. Dawood's father had developed a friendship with Mastan and Lala during his service in the police force and he remained friends with them even after he retired.

Dawood's ambition to make it big saw him opening an electronics goods store in Manish Market, still sometimes referred to as Mumbai's grey goods supermarket. Along with his trade of pushing smuggled electronics, Dawood also had a finger in the extortion pie. With brother Sabir in tow, he went around demanding protection money or maliciously wrecking shops belonging to other businessmen dealing in smuggled goods in Manish Market and elsewhere.

Even as a youth, Dawood had believed in the expansion of businesses, and so he tried his hand at conning people too, often selling them a watch or an expensive piece of jewellery and switching it with a stone or rock in the final seconds of the transaction.

Sabir was the unofficial first member of what went on to become the D-Company (and very briefly the

Young Party). The party's first major haul came in 1974 when Dawood hit upon the idea of hijacking a private courier, or *angadia*, as they are called in Mumbai. Back then, if large sums of money had to be sent from one person to another, a carrier would be hired to quickly ferry the cash across. The angadias embarked on their journeys unprotected, and Dawood realized that they would be relatively simple targets that would yield maximum gains.

And so, in December that year, Dawood and his gang of seven faithful cronies decided to waylay an angadia after a tip-off about its route. Despite the clumsy execution, the octet managed to decamp with a large sum of money that they were to later realize was around Rs 4.75 lakh, belonging to the Corporation Bank. The Pydhonie police registered the case as the biggest bank robbery till date. After lying low for a while, Dawood and Sabir came out of hiding as changed men. They were now powerful. This is believed to be the moment that turned Dawood the thug into Dawood the don.

Unfortunately, Sabir's days of thunder were slowly drawing to a close, partly because Dawood and he had made too many enemies and partly because they had been living just too dangerously. After kick-starting a feud with the Pathan brothers—Amirzada and Alamzeb—the duo employed the services of gangster

Manya Surve in 1981 to help them get their revenge. But as it turned out, Sabir's car was followed to a petrol station where he had pulled over. The Pathan brothers made the most of the opportunity and, along with their associates, ambushed Sabir and pummelled his body with bullets.

The murder shocked Mumbai's civilians and policemen alike and created ripples within the underworld. With Sabir lying in his grave, Dawood took over the reins of the Young Party/D-Company and subsequently the gang. A few years down the line, Dawood had made quite a reputation for himself as a hot-blooded and violent young man who had laid waste the business interests of numerous non-cooperative shop owners and other businessmen.

The downside of this, of course, was that Dawood and his tiny band of acquaintances were beginning to attract the attention of the police. Tales of his methods of extortion and the mayhem he was capable of unleashing were making the police nervous. It is believed in some circles that being the son of a constable made the police even more determined to bring him to justice.

This is where the Mumbai chapter of the then fledgling D-Company came to a sharp and sudden close, with the young Dawood hurriedly setting off for greener pastures—Dubai. Having landed in Dubai, the don set about putting his house in order. He gave his lieutenants, corporals and foot soldiers a single order—wind up your business affairs and occupations, and leave for Dubai.

The urgency of Dawood's message was not lost on his minions who began trooping across to the Gulf. Two of Dawood's closest and most powerful aides at one point were Rajendra Sadashiv Nikhalje and Shakeel Babumiya Shaikh, better known as Chhota Rajan and Chhota Shakeel respectively. Rajan arrived in Dubai nearly a year before Shakeel, giving him that much more time to ingratiate himself with Dawood. Shakeel answered the D-Company head honcho's call sometime in 1988 and came to Dubai to find Rajan enjoying the power, responsibility and privilege that came with being Dawood's right-hand man. For all his hard work and efforts to please the D-Company's leader, Shakeel had to spend a few years picking up the scraps.

Gradually, Dawood's little group expanded into a vast empire that had its fingers in all sorts of dirty pies, ranging from extortion rackets to smuggling, and even the Hindi film industry. At one point, it was fair to say that Dawood's empire was almost the underworld equivalent of the business holdings of the Ambanis, Tatas and Birlas.

The don bought himself a massive mansion in Dubai and christened it White House. Decades later, *Forbes* magazine would confirm the notion that Dawood had about himself by proclaiming him to be one of the most powerful people in the world—almost up there with the President of the USA. Sitting comfortably in his heavily guarded mansion, Dawood would remote control proceedings in India with a few people on the ground.

Anis, in the meantime, was riding on the notoriety and fear that his brother, Dawood, evoked. He was part of the gang, but preferred to have his own people and lieutenants working for him. He focused on property encroachment, and extortion from builders and film producers—businesses that made him very rich. Salem's smuggling business also became a lucrative part of Anis's portfolio.

By the time the 1990s rolled in, the D-Company's grip on Mumbai was gradually tightening and all was well for Dawood and his men—until Babri Masjid and the communal riots that followed. The reaction of Muslims in Mumbai was like a slap across Dawood's face. One Muslim woman reportedly sent Dawood a box of broken bangles, that worst insult for a man, for it ridiculed his inability as a man to protect fellow Muslims. That was the straw that broke the camel's back and brought the D-Company to a crossroads. The gang's next step would be the one that determined its future course.

Pakistan's premier intelligence agency, the Inter-Services Intelligence (ISI), was now truly salivating. It had been waiting for such an opportunity and here it was on a silver platter. For years, the ISI policy in its Kashmir operations had been to 'prick and bleed'. Now, the plan was to make a 'deep incision' in the heart of the nation's psyche. But in order to execute this plan, the ISI would need some people on the ground as executioners.

In addition to groups like the Palestinian Liberation Organization and Afghan Mujahideen, the ISI contacted various wealthy Dubai-based businessmen, as well as Dawood, Anis, Mohammad Dossa, Tiger Memon, Tahir Merchant and a number of other Indian dons, briefing them about their latest operation: *Tehreek-e-Inteqaam* (the initiative of revenge).

Until now, the Company had been a dangerous bunch, but they had done nothing to sport the tag of 'terrorists'. All that was about to change as Dawood called a meeting at his White House to set his plan into motion. Blood begets blood and violence begets violence, they reasoned. And began planning for retribution.

Indian Muslim youths were flown over to Pakistan where they received demolition and ammunition training. They were then flown across to Dubai and turned into brainwashed tools for jihad, with hours and hours of video footage of Muslim women being raped in the Gujarat riots of 1992 following the demolition of the mosque. These young, heat-seeking missiles were now ready for launch.

It was decided that Tiger Memon, a Dawood aide

from Mahim who was part of the inner coterie—and the top gold and silver smuggler—would be the kingpin. Memon and Dossa were to spearhead the operation. Dawood would provide logistical support to Memon to bring the 'raw material' to Indian shores. Memon brought over eight tonnes of RDX, thousands of grenades and a number of Kalashnikov rifles to the coast of Raigad, Maharashtra, in February 1993. The stage was set and the actors were all but ready for the grand finale. Memon had assembled a team of nineteen people to carry out what would be the most destructive series of bomb attacks in India.

On 12 March 1993, in a little over two hours, ten bomb explosions were set off all over Mumbai, scarring the face of the city. Starting off around 1.28 p.m. at the Bombay Stock Exchange building, explosions occurred at the Air India Tower, the grain market at Masjid Bunder, Plaza cinema hall, Sena Bhavan in Dadar, the passport office in Worli and five-star hotels in Bandra and Santa Cruz. If that weren't enough, grenades were also hurled at the airport and the Mahim Fishermen's Colony.

Around 257 people died and 700 were injured, some grievously. Through keen deduction and a lot of good luck, most of the Mumbai Police's biggest breakthroughs came in the very first hour after the explosions. After working overtime with the few leads that they had, various branches of the city's police force began unravelling the conspiracy and planning that went into the execution of Black Friday. One hundred and twenty-nine accused were identified by the police, but the chief conspirators—Memon and Dawood—were nowhere to be found.

The aftermath of this serial bomb attack was manifold. The Indian media exposed the level of the D-Company's involvement in the attacks and the fact that Hindus and Muslims alike were killed in this so-called act of vengeance. Public perception was polarized now and people were baying for the blood of Dawood and his cronies. There was disarray within the Company itself, with Dawood's right-hand man Rajan feeling the twinge of disillusionment, which slowly intensified into a burning disagreement with what the gang had just done.

Meanwhile, over in Dubai, things were getting a little hairy at the White House, with the Indian government trying to hammer out an extradition treaty with the United Arab Emirates government. The Gulf, which until then had been a sanctuary for fugitive expatriates, seemed to have been compromised. Numerous fugitive expats began to panic and feel insecure. Dawood, however, had his eyes on a fresh start.

After considering a number of locations, Dawood realized that the ISI would keep him and his people safe. So, around the end 1994, Dawood began once again to shift his empire to a new land. Karachi would be the new home of the D-Company. The port city bore more than a passing resemblance to Mumbai, and Dawood and company were able to seamlessly slip into life in Pakistan.

SIX

SCURRYING FOR COVER

THE CITY AND ITS POLICE WERE caught completely off guard by the 1993 blasts. Salem had gone to offer his Friday prayers and from there went to his Santa Cruz office. After an otherwise uneventful day at work, he left for home in Jogeshwari around 3 p.m. and saw first-hand the turmoil the city had been hurled into.

By the time Salem reached home, it was clear that the explosions were the handiwork of a terrorist organization. Salem was reminded of the arms and ammunition he had delivered to Sanjay Dutt's residence barely a month ago. It didn't take him very long to connect the dots.

Soon, the police launched a major crackdown. Perpetrators were being picked up from all over the city. Even the rich and famous were not spared. The arrests of

Hanif Kadawala, Samir Hingora, Baba Moosa Chauhan, Manzoor Ahmed and others led Salem to believe that he could be the next. He decided to flee to a safer destination before he was trapped in the clutches of the Mumbai Police.

Salem had begun to believe that he had finally settled down in life. He had been in Mumbai for barely seven or eight years and had already carved a niche for himself in the underworld. His business of smuggling and *bhaigiri* was flourishing—an office in Mumbai, a car, a gang of over twenty like-minded lads, plenty of respect from those in his village and, most of all, money had ceased to be a problem. It had been a couple of years since his wedding. Sameera had begun teaching him English and a little bit about the etiquette and customs of the civilized world. But the serial blasts and the arrests of his friends had shattered his newfound image of success.

There was an added dilemma about whether or not Sameera should join him. He consulted his friends, especially Kalam, and they all advised him that it would not be wise to travel with her. If the police were to detain them, it would unnecessarily put poor Sameera in an uncomfortable situation. So Salem decided to travel alone to Delhi, then to Lucknow so that he could make a fake passport bearing a different name for himself. He planned on relocating to Dubai and having Sameera join him later.

SEVEN

DESPAIR IN DUBAI

ABU SALEM KNEW, AS HE ENTERED Dubai airport, that he would not be returning to Mumbai any time soon. He was by now familiar with Dubai airport as he had been to the city four times since launching his smuggling career in 1987. But he had never anticipated that he'd be planning a long sojourn there.

Dubai might have been described as a city whose pavements were tiled with gold, but Salem found no such thing anywhere in the United Arab Emirates. On his earlier visits, he had found it to be populated with Indians, Pakistanis, Bangladeshis and even Filipinos. There were more high-rises in Nariman Point and Cuffe Parade in the south of Mumbai than in the whole of Dubai. Until 1991, Dubai had only one skyscraper. It seemed like long stretches of desert on shining, clean roads. He had wondered why all the bhais had decided to move to Dubai and why so many film stars fancied this place. He'd seen people returning from Dubai with their pockets overflowing with cash, but frankly, this place with all its squalor and filth looked no better than Bhendi Bazaar.

Aziz had convinced him that moving to Dubai would be the perfect way to work closely with Dawood and Anis, and get closer to the centre of operations. The way the fledgling gangster saw it, if Anis was Dawood's right-hand man, Salem had to try and make himself Anis's right-hand man, and that would make him Dawood's 'left-hand man'. To Salem's ambitious mind, the logic seemed flawless.

The young man managed to get a small place for himself at Yusuf Bakar Road in a suburb of Dubai which he shared with three aides of Anis Ibrahim. It was located in the Oont Bazaar (Camel Market) area and was separated from Dubai proper by a creek. Oont Bazaar had been set up in the early 1970s as a market for the sale of cattle. Since camels were the most popular form of cattle in this part of the world, the market became their fiefdom, so to speak.

One could generally get from Dubai city to Oont Bazaar and back via something called *abra* (the local ferry) that cost around 25 Arab Emirate dirhams. Salem had been told that it was the quickest and cheapest means of transport there. Oont Bazaar was not just remotely located, its narrow, dingy lanes also had an acrid, musty smell. It was a disgusting mix of grime, sweaty body odour and the filthy stench of camels and cattle. Salem often wondered how the locals could stomach it.

Unfortunately, he had no choice about his location. Interpol, the Crime Branch, the Intelligence Bureau (IB) and everyone in between was baying for his blood and this was the only place he could inhabit inconspicuously. But, as they say, every cloud has a silver lining and this hovel became a source of great fascination to Salem. He realized it could become a brilliant hideout for people fleeing India and looking for a safe house to lie low in. First of all, it was inexpensive and inconspicuous and so the people hiding there would be able to slip below the radar. Secondly, Oont Bazaar was an acquired taste and there was no chance that the authorities would be able to handle that dreadful stench for long enough to search the whole hotel. This seemed like the recipe for a perfect hideout.

He was, however, getting increasingly worried about how he would bring Sameera there. With him gone, he knew she would be harassed by the Indian authorities. Of course, bringing her to live in Oont Bazaar was not an option, especially the hovel he called home during his initial days there. Finally, temporary arrangements were made for the lad from Azamgarh to live in Bar Dubai on the first floor of the building that housed Anis's video company—King's Video. The video tape business was massive there. People loved films and loved the stars. Not just the Indians, but even the Pakistanis and Bangladeshis were crazily attracted to Bollywood stars. No wonder Bollywood's finest flocked so regularly to perform or just relax there.

With a respectable roof over his head, Salem knew it was now time to restart his life in Dubai in exactly the same way as he had turned his life around after moving to Mumbai. All it had taken was a few short years. Back then, he had had nothing but his determination and never-say-die attitude. Today, he was armed with an innate understanding of the art of managing the underworld and turning people's fear and insecurity into cold, hard cash.

Salem had landed in Dubai under the name and fictitious identity of Akil Ahmed Azmi. He had had fake passports made in Lucknow for himself and Sameera under the names of Akil Ahmed Azmi and Sabina Azmi. It was this masterstroke that saved Salem from being extradited to India from Dubai, despite continuous pressure from the Indian government. The Arab bureaucracy maintained that there was no one called Abu Salem in the United Arab Emirates.

The ploy was later perfected by Pakistan as well. When the Indian government sent complete dossiers with personal details and even the Pakistani address of Dawood Ibrahim, the Pakistani government claimed that there was no Dawood Ibrahim Kaskar on Pakistani soil. The Indians must have mistaken Shaikh Dawood for their most wanted accused, they scoffed at the Indian bureaucrats.

Once Salem left the shores of Mumbai, he would formally never again be known as Abu Salem Abdul Qayyum Ansari. He would use his various fake identities for residential, business and travel purposes. But whenever he needed to spread terror, intimidate people and demand money, he would always return to his old greeting: *'Abu Salem bol raha hoon.'*

EIGHT

FIRST BLOOD

17 FEBRUARY 1995 WILL REMAIN FOREVER etched in Jyoti Pradeep Jain's memory.

As she and her husband Pradeep Jain were eating a quiet dinner in their Andheri residence, the telephone began to ring. She stood up from the table and walked over to the phone. The call would change her destiny.

On the line was a man who identified himself as Abu Salem from Dubai and asked to speak to her brother-in-law Ashok Jain. When Jyoti said Ashok was not home, the man asked who was available. Jyoti answered honestly. Salem then asked to speak to Pradeep Jain.

Jyoti watched as her husband took the phone and began to get steadily worked up. She had never seen her husband get so angry. He hung up, tense and stressed out. When Jyoti asked him what was wrong, he explained that it was a gangster called Abu Salem trying to pressurize Pradeep to leave his Koldongri property or be prepared to pay for it with his life. Frightened, Jyoti asked him to approach the police, but Pradeep refused.

Settled in Dubai, Salem was planning to expand his work and to establish himself as a powerful don in the city. Anis had given carte blanche to Salem and asked him to take over the business of Bollywood and builders. Salem's only brief was to 'generate money through whatever means'. Following these instructions, Salem had unleashed scouts and confidants everywhere to sniff out lucrative business deals and affluent business people making their millions quietly, all potential targets. One of Salem's primary reconnaissance agents was Riyaz Siddiqui. His only role was to provide accurate and reliable information on the businessmen. He helped Salem zero in on targets and seal large extortion pay-offs.

The biggest target that Riyaz had provided so far was a builder by the name of Ashok Jain. The Jain family lived in the two-storey Brijkamal Bungalow at Gulmohar JVPD. They were five brothers—Suresh, Ashok, Rakesh, Pradeep and Sunil. They had a construction business, Kamla Constructions, with its office occupying the ground floor of their bungalow.

When Salem called Ashok Jain and threatened him, he buckled fast under pressure. Ashok was quite well off and it seemed perfectly reasonable that he be made to pay Rs 10 lakh a month, Salem told him politely. He obliged Salem's gang in the first month. But at the end of the second month, the monthly instalment was missing. Apparently, his brother Pradeep had convinced Ashok to stop the payments.

Pradeep was one of those people who did not fear the underworld. Whether out of misguided bravado or a hunch that the mafia was bluffing, he refused to be intimidated to shell out so much as a single paisa. Salem called Riyaz and asked him to go and put some sense into Ashok and threaten Pradeep. Riyaz explained to Ashok that a man like Salem was dangerous and not to be trifled with. The fact that he was working for Anis Ibrahim Kaskar and the D-Company, he continued, was further reason to take him very seriously. No one refused the demands of the D-Company unless they were impatiently awaiting their own funeral. But Riyaz's arguments were all in vain. The Jain brothers refused to budge.

This presented a predicament for Salem and his boys. If one solitary builder got away without paying, the others would surely turn cocky. Another builder would call Salem's bluff and decide not to pay. Then a third would follow and so on. Soon, no one would take the underworld seriously. There would be no more money for the D-Company, just mockery.

So Salem concluded that blood would have to be spilled. Even if just one of the five Jain brothers was bumped off, it would spread waves of terror through Mumbai's business community. Ashok was called one last time, for a final warning. The phone rang and Ashok promptly answered. Salem was shell-shocked to hear Pradeep snatching the phone from his brother and screaming expletives down the phone at him. Very few had spoken to Salem with such disdain ever since he joined the Company.

When Anis took over the conversation, Pradeep launched a volley of verbal abuse at him as well, reiterating that they would not pay. After the phone call was over, Salem looked at a crestfallen Anis and felt the need to salvage the pride both he and his mentor had lost in that conversation. In Salem's mind it was now clear as crystal—Pradeep was the Jain brother who would have to die.

This was not about money any more. It was a matter of the Company's clout and respect in Mumbai. A message was immediately sent to Salem's driver Mohammad Mehndi Hassan (aka Sunny) in Kolhapur. He was told that Salim Haddi was to be taken to Pradeep Jain's office and he was to be executed. To ensure that the task was completed, Salem sweetened the deal for his men. He told Sunny that if Pradeep was killed, he would give them an incentive of Rs 1 lakh each. The weapons were delivered near a hotel in Bhendi Bazaar. All preparations were in place.

It's only in the movies that mafia hitmen roam around with their weapons tucked in the small of their backs. Real-life hitmen, in fact, are provided guns just before the hit, by an errand boy. This courier boy was assigned the task of collecting the gun from the manager and passing it on to the shooter. Since each automatic Star pistol was valued at around Rs 1 lakh, mafia bosses hardly wanted to let these be kept with gunmen who could lose them or be arrested. Smuggling and procurement of weapons remained a difficult task, so it was prudent to keep the weapons circulating.

Once Haddi was given the weapon, all Salem had to do was sit back and wait for the phone to ring. Haddi conducted the recce and studied Pradeep Jain's movements. It took a couple of weeks for Haddi to decide on the most opportune moment to strike. On 7 March 1995, Salem received the phone call he had been eagerly awaiting. Haddi called to say that he had barged into Pradeep's office with his cohorts, looked him straight in the eye and shot him dead. Pradeep's younger brother, Sunil, who was present in the office, had also suffered injuries. Was he still defiant, even as death looked him in the eye, Salem asked Haddi. The ace shooter replied in the affirmative. The phone clicked as Salem hung up.

For Salem, Pradeep's killing was punishment for the impudence he had dared to show Salem and his boss. Jyoti's whole world, on the other hand, had come crashing down. She had married Pradeep in 1982 and her thirteen years of married life had been blissful. Salem had destroyed everything.

On 20 March 1995, while Jyoti was sitting at a prayer meeting to mark her husband's *terahvaan* (the thirteenth day after death), she received a call. The caller asked her name, she identified herself as Jyoti, Pradeep's wife. She assumed it was possibly a business associate of Pradeep or maybe even a distant relative or friend who had failed to make it to the final rites and was calling to convey condolences.

The caller, instead, said, *'Abu Salem bol raha hoon'* and then began laughing hysterically. When he stopped, he asked if she was enjoying her widowhood. He told her that Pradeep would still have been alive had he only paid up.

Jyoti was furious and asked what he wanted. 'Now tell your brothers-in-law to pay up or I will kill all of them, one by one,' Salem said. Jyoti slammed the phone down full of rage and fear. When her brother-in-law, Sunil, inquired about the caller, she just said 'Abu Salem' and began crying uncontrollably.

Pradeep Jain's killing had frightened his brothers. Sunil was initially hell-bent on approaching the police, but gave up the idea after he was reminded of the consequences. They agreed that they would resume payments, but there was a snag. They had a cash-flow problem and would be unable to make cash payments. Salem didn't think much of it at the time and instead told them to give him some flats in the building they were constructing. After all, property nearly always appreciated in value, especially in a city like Mumbai and could easily be sold off for cash at a later date. It was at this time that he hit upon the marvellous idea of accepting flats as payment, if cash was unavailable.

In 2006, the Indian government managed to secure Salem's extradition from Portugal on eight cases, two of which were handled by the Mumbai Police. The Pradeep Jain murder case was one of the strongest cases against him. In the 2008 trial in Mumbai, it was Jyoti's detailed testimony that was to prove to be one of the most important one against Salem.

NINE

SALEM'S KILLING MACHINES

CONTRACT KILLINGS, OR *SUPARI* HITS, WERE considered a rather respectable profession in the Mumbai mafia through the 1980s and all the way till the late 1990s. The professionals would demand a hefty sum to kill a designated target in Mumbai; it was a truly lucrative business. There were two kinds of supari jobs. The first was a straight assignment, in which a business rival or relative wanted someone killed and was willing to foot the bill.

The second was punishment killing, usually done at the behest of a mob boss. Traditionally, this treatment was meted out to business tycoons, assorted moneybags or friends of enemies, anybody who refused to meet the conditions laid down by a gangster. The consequence of their defiance was that they would pay with their lives. In either case, the idea behind the killing was simply to put on a display of brute power.

One of the most talked about supari killings in the 1980s was that of Amirzada, Dawood Ibrahim's arch-enemy and the boss of the Pathan syndicate. Amirzada had earned Dawood's enmity because of his involvement in Dawood's brother Sabir Kaskar's death. Since Amirzada had already been arrested and was going through trials and court hearings, Dawood decided to have him killed dramatically in the court premises. Dawood picked Pardesi for the job and offered him a pay-off of Rs 50,000. The sum was so exorbitant in those days that it was the subject of animated discussion in police and underworld circles for years.

It was much later that Dawood began using the police to eliminate his rivals in fake encounters. This method of settling scores was arguably a lot more economical and effective for the don. Until then, two pairs of shooters had become quite famous in Dawood's gang—B2 and S2. Baba Gabriel and Bachchi Pandey were called Two Bee or B Square or B2.

These ferocious shooters had executed many assignments for Dawood in the late 1980s and early 1990s. Their targets were not just people in Mumbai, but also scattered across Delhi, Uttar Pradesh and Gujarat. Former Mumbai Police Commissioner Amarjeet Singh

Samra did not rest until he chased them out of the Mumbai–Thane region, spelling the end of B2's era in the Mumbai underworld.

Dawood's gang then saw the emergence of two deadlier assassins named S2—Sunil Sawant, alias Sautya, and Subhash Singh Thakur. They were considered killing machines, and sometimes referred to as 'the undertakers'. Since the Mumbai mafia had begun using sophisticated weaponry in the 1990s, including Kalashnikov rifles, Sautya and Thakur both began using the AK-47 to eliminate their victims.

The sharpshooter received a lot of respect and clout. The boss gave direct assignments to these killer squads and often rewarded them handsomely. In those days, every high-profile killing was planned by two pairs of shooters. The A team and B team comprised a main shooter and a supporting shooter. The idea was to have two teams of shooters so that there could be backup in case the primary team failed and so that someone could watch the main shooter's back.

As they gained in experience and won the confidence of the boss, the B team would be elevated to A team status. Everyone wanted to be promoted to the rank of sharpshooter in the gang. Some were natural hitmen, fearless while shooting and skilled at making a neat escape, while others were born disasters.

Anil Parab, alias Wangya, one of Dawood's ace

shooters, was among those who aspired to become a hitman, but his first assignment had bombed badly. He had been entrusted the task of silencing a witness, Hansraj Shah, in Vikhroli court and had totally failed. He could not make his mark as a hitman until he teamed up with Sautya. However, this partnership did not do well either and it was only when he partnered Subhash Singh Thakur that Sautya struck top form.

Once he moved to Dubai, Salem knew that he needed ace sharpshooters who could work for him as enforcers just as the men Dawood had once employed. It was convenient to have a dozen boys do his bidding, but the responsibility of conducting a recce, identifying a target, keeping a watch on the quarry and then finally moving in for the kill was a different ball game altogether. Ten street ruffians did not have the ability to do what a single trained assassin could. And a gang's reputation was built on the ferocity of its sharpshooters.

The first deadly shooter to join Salem's gang was Salim Shaikh, alias Salim Haddi. Salim is a common Muslim name and the underworld had its fair share of Salims. So to distinguish them they were given an additional title. So, for example, if one Salim had driven a tempo before joining the gang, he was named Salim Tempo. Another Salim who specialized in the fake passport business was called Salim Passport. Salim Bismillah Khan who lived in Kurla, also an accused in the serial blasts case, came to be known as Salim Kurla. One Salim who had used a sword in booth capturing in South Mumbai for a Congress candidate earned the title of Salim Talwar. There were half a dozen more Salims who were employed in the underworld and had similarly strange titles.

Salim Shaikh, or Salim Haddi, had been a jobless and desperate young man. He was living in abject poverty and his family was on the verge of starvation. A school dropout, Salim was a reed-thin youth with a prominent Adam's apple which became more pronounced whenever he was nervous or stressed. He faced humiliation everywhere until he was given a job as a hitman by Salem.

He was named Salim Haddi because *haddi* is Hindi for bone. The epithet couldn't have been more apt. Salim seemed to have no flesh on his body, only bones. This youth became one of the most dreaded sharpshooters in the underworld and thus became more notorious than all his namesakes.

However, since Salem modelled himself on Dawood, he was keen to find a killing partner for Haddi. But no one really fit the bill. This went on for a while until finally, the Mumbai Police provided Salem with a once-in-a-lifetime opportunity. Constable Rajesh Igwe, of Local Arms (LA) Division-II at Naigaon, had been suspended from service for dereliction of duty. Igwe was an alcoholic and despite being given commando training, always reported late for duty.

Very few policemen were trained in handling sophisticated weapons, and Igwe was among those few commando cops who were comfortable with guns of any calibre. His unprofessional behaviour and lack of discipline though had earned him the wrath of his superiors. Normally, temporary suspension from duty worked as a deterrent for most cops as it not only meant loss of face among colleagues but also a loss of nearly 25 per cent of salary. But Igwe was intransigent. Nothing could tame or reform him, and it was just a suspension.

As police constables from LA-II wing were normally posted on escort duty, to ferry criminals from jail to courts and back, they were in frequent contact with criminals from several gangs. It was during the course of one of those escort duties for a member of Salem's gang that Igwe heard that the gang's leader was looking for a sharpshooter.

Soon after his suspension, Igwe began to get desperate for money and decided to get in touch with Salem in Dubai and offer his services. Salem was waiting for this opportunity and immediately inducted Igwe into his gang, thereby becoming the first mafia don to have a serving policeman work for him as a sharpshooter. The trend would be followed by Amar Naik much later who began hiring suspended or dismissed policemen as gang members.

Thus, the Haddi–Igwe duo unleashed terror in the city. Igwe's background as a policeman proved to be immensely helpful in conducting recce missions and avoiding the police dragnet. And they killed several high-profile people leaving the city's police baffled at their temerity. The duo's successful run boosted Salem's stock in the underworld by several notches. His bosses were pleased with his work and his peers had begun feeling jealous about his rising notoriety and growing menace in the city. Later on, Salem would recruit a bigger army of shooters, but Igwe remained the jewel in his crown and his recruitment into the mafia was a real coup—a police officer suddenly jumps ship and begins working for the underworld; you couldn't make up a more incredible story if you wanted to.

TEN

SALEM IMPORTS RENT-A-KILLER

PRADEEP JAIN'S KILLING HAD ANNOUNCED THE arrival of Salem on the underworld scene. Whenever Salem called anyone, he'd mention casually that Jain had been punished for his impudence and that the same fate could befall them too if they didn't fall in line. The builders in question would instantly pay up.

Very soon, the builder community started paying up without any negotiations or even a perfunctory struggle. Salem started filling the coffers of Anis Ibrahim which had begun to dry up. Both Dawood and Anis were extremely pleased with Salem's progress. Within the span of a year, Salem had not only managed to get himself deeply entrenched in the underworld but also vastly increased the income of the D-Company.

Salem soon got an office near Naif Road in Deira, Dubai, after the twelfth-floor office in Pearl Tower. Anis already had King's Video in Dubai. Salem went ahead and opened a car showroom in Karamah and called it King of Cars. Salem got five bungalows in the swanky neighbourhood of Jumeirah Beach. He began using one as a residence, the other as an office, and the remaining three were rented out

Soon, he became a law unto himself. He was given total freedom to operate as he wanted. He could pick and choose any victim; he could summon any businessman to Dubai to extract money or torment him. Salem's success, though, had actually been a major fluke. There was no method to his madness or finely developed strategy behind his success.

It was partly out of frustration and partly out of an unending need to impress Anis that Salem began calling random rich people in Mumbai and threatening them. Buoyed by the fact that his first few threats had ended successfully, Salem began having weapons sent to Mumbai from Nepal. These weapons would be for the motley crew of shooters he was slowly assembling.

The modus operandi for the hits was to get a message across to Salim Haddi who had become Salem's top man for the job. Salim Haddi would immediately rush to a phone booth in Chembur and call Salem for the details of the hit or scare. While Salem was busy conveying his boss's 'requirements' to builders, film producers, industrialists, etc., Salim Haddi would be mobilizing shooters for the job. If the targets—as these builders, film producers and industrialists were referred to—refused to comply, shooters were sent over to their office. Often, the targets buckled and agreed to pay up via hawala transactions. If the targets failed to comply, they would be killed. It was rather simple.

Finally, Salem began to be accorded the sort of respect he felt he deserved from his boss, Anis. The latter was so pleased with all the money that Salem was earning for him and the terror he was spreading in his name that the fledgling gangster who had begun taking big strides in the underworld slowly became Anis Ibrahim's blue-eyed boy. Not everything changed, however. Anis continued to order Salem to mix a drink or fetch a cup of tea, even in front of other guests. But Salem swallowed his pride and remained loyal to his master.

The next major hit that Salem scored after Pradeep Jain was the killing of Chembur builder Om Prakash Kukreja. Kukreja was shot dead on 18 September 1995 in his office in the north-eastern suburb of Mumbai. Subsequently, a relative of Kukreja's travelled to Dubai and paid Rs 1 crore to Salem for providing amnesty to others in the Kukreja clan. The killing of Kukreja really shook the Mumbai builder community.

Now, Ranjit Singh Sharma, who was then the joint

commissioner of police (crime), and Rakesh Maria, who was the deputy commissioner of police, decided to take on the growing menace of the Salem gang. The gang's shooters were shortlisted and killed in police encounters. Haddi and Igwe, both ace shooters, were killed within weeks of Kukreja's murder. The idea was to not only curb the growing terror of Salem's gang but also send a message to others not to join him. For a while, many shooters felt jittery and nervous.

Salem knew that it would be difficult to groom another pair of shooters like Haddi and Igwe. Additionally, shooters were quite expensive and their maintenance took a massive toll on the gang's finances and resources. If these shooters were to be arrested, Salem would have to spend money on their legal defence and pay for the upkeep of their families. For Salem, once the shooter was picked up by the police, he was reduced to the status of a non-performing asset and any kind of further expenses on him would be seen as zero return on investment.

From his days as a smuggler, Salem had preferred businesses that required low investment and zero maintenance. He now came up with an unconventional idea that not only revolutionized the contract killing business in the city but also threw a major challenge to the Mumbai Police.

Salem got in touch with his cousins and relatives back

home in Sarai Mir and asked them to look for boys who were unemployed, keen on travelling to Mumbai, hungry to earn a decent wage without working too hard and had the guts to do anything that was asked of them. Salem was very keenly aware of the poverty and desperation in the villages where even a daily earning of Rs 100 was regarded as substantial income. Also, these village boys were full of bravado and were willing to get violent at the slightest provocation. Most of them had also wielded country-made revolvers or handguns in skirmishes.

Salem decided to import these desperadoes to Mumbai. Their job would entail shooting a victim from point-blank range and escaping immediately thereafter. He was then supposed to return the gun to the person who had given it to him and board the Gorakhpur Express the next day. Salem promised a return railway ticket and a cash reward of Rs 5000 for such jobs. Even if these youths were arrested, Salem neither had to foot their legal bills nor did he have to financially support the family. 'I can get boys to kill anyone in Mumbai for a remuneration of just Rs 5000. If they fail, I don't lose anything. If they succeed, I get the job done for loose change,' Salem apparently told his people in Dubai.

For Salem, Rs 5000 may have been petty cash but for the villager it was enough money to kill someone. Suddenly, Salem had a surfeit of boys willing to pull the trigger at his command. The police were baffled by these new entrants into the killing business. These youths had no previous record, no roots in Mumbai, came from nowhere and vanished into thin air after the killing. Never mind the shooters, the police could not even locate the middlemen or any other links to the killing. For several months, the Mumbai Police groped in the dark until they managed to nab one of the shooters who had come to kill a top film director, and thus the beans were spilled.

There was another variation added to the mix. In the past, seasoned errand boys or experienced courier guys were assigned the task of delivering the weapons to the shooters. However, now Salem decided to use poor Muslim women as couriers for the gang. These women were either widows of his men (who had been killed by the police) or relatives of his people. Out of fear of Salem, they went ahead and did the job and also got paid. The only difference was that Salem was paying them a fraction of what he had paid experienced delivery men.

It was a fantastic idea that paid dividends, and Salem managed to implement it as long as his village had no shortage of willing youths. An unlettered man, Salem had introduced to the underworld the concept of 'disposable' assassins. It was the perfect example of 'single-use' killers. This earned him further brownie points with his bosses.

ELEVEN

TAMING BOLLYWOOD

BACK IN THE 1990S, BOLLYWOOD WAS nothing like the sanitized, studio-controlled, corporate-financed industry it is today. Tinsel town had its moguls and its mandarins who, along with Mumbai's realty players, controlled incredible sums of black money. So it was only natural that when Salem decided to go beyond the construction business, it would be to the veritable gold mine of Bollywood.

The first target would be Subhash Ghai, one of the reigning maharajas of superstardom. Ghai's cash registers had been ringing and coffers overflowing ever since his 1993 box office superhit *Khalnayak*, starring Salem's now-on, now-off friend Sanjay Dutt. The director's stocks had soared so much that he could even sign Shah Rukh Khan for a film.

This, Salem believed, was the perfect time to send Bollywood a message. And the target would be Ghai. Salem deputed five youths from Azamgarh to deliver this 'hit'. But the deputy commissioner of police, Zone VII, Satyapal Singh, received intelligence about the hit squad. He immediately assigned the task of foiling the attack to his special squad, led by Assistant Inspector Pradeep Sharma. The police team laid a trap and arrested the quintet of would-be killers.

Salem, on his part, continues to maintain that he had never intended to kill the director. All he wanted was to send out a message to him. And that missive was: 'Pay up now or be prepared to face dire consequences.' Later, Ghai said in an interview that Salem had called him and spoken to him quite politely. Salem wanted the foreign rights for his movie *Pardes* and when Ghai told him that it had already been signed away, Salem asked for a print of the movie so that he could make pirated copies and sell them. Salem also reportedly told Ghai that he was a big fan of his work.

Salem's other target in Bollywood was director Rajiv Rai, who had seen major commercial success with *Tridev* (starring Naseeruddin Shah and Sunny Deol), *Mohra* (starring Akshay Kumar and Raveena Tandon) and *Gupt* (starring Bobby Deol and Kajol). As it turned out, Rai was a far easier man to convince than Ghai.

One day, Salem received an annoying phone call from a news reporter who worked with the *Indian Express*. Audaciously, the reporter asked Salem if his men were so incompetent that they couldn't even deliver on a single death threat. The gangster said simply that it had never really been his intention to kill either Ghai or Rai. He added that the following week would see someone killed.

The next week came along and, sure enough, the gangster delivered on his word. Gulshan Kumar was brutally killed in public. The killing would also become Salem's big ticket into the heart of Bollywood. After the Gulshan Kumar murder, the *Indian Express* reporter called Salem again. 'Was this the murder you were talking about?'

But this time, the bluster was missing on the other end of the line. The Indian government was furious about this high-profile murder and the mafiosi was getting jittery. The whole of the Dawood gang was running scared, tails between their legs.

Salem hesitated for a moment and when he did speak, it was to say, '*Yeh murder Lal Krishna Advani ne karvaya hai*, why don't you call and ask him?' So, Salem did not own up to the Gulshan Kumar murder; nevertheless, he had managed to generate a deep-rooted fear psychosis in the film industry. Filmwallahs had a simple logic: If this man could make someone like Ghai cower and could bump off a big fish like Gulshan Kumar, no one was safe.

Salem had begun to use a code name when he called film personalities: Captain. The Mumbai Police had begun tapping phones, and since these conversations were considered to be culpable evidence, Salem decided to use the code name. The industry was soon abuzz about calls from the Captain.

Salem also appointed a small army of spies and scouts in the industry, people who were keeping tabs on a wide range of industry insiders. The most famous among them was a producer called Bobby. This man could walk into any Bollywood office, meet any star and demand a commitment. 'At one point of time, some thirty top film stars had signed contracts with Bobby. They had promised chunks of dates to Bobby and there was no hassle about the remuneration,' recalls a top film director. Even some top stars who routinely played hookey after committing dates with reputed banners and haggled endlessly over their signing amount and fee would heed hastily when that one call came from the Captain, followed sometimes by a polite threat from Bobby. Suddenly, they would all be available, usually gratis.

Soon, all of Bollywood's biggest names were inhabitants of Salem's cell phone book. And whenever they flew to a European destination to shoot a scene or a song, they would invariably fly into Dubai to pay obeisance to him in person. Without exception. But none of them met anyone called Salem.

The mafia boss's modus operandi was to meet Bollywood's who's who as Arsalan (a fictional assistant to Abu Salem). This man was a suave and elegant person with a sophisticated, polite and urbane manner, while the reputation of Abu Salem was that of a ferocious, bloodthirsty don whose language was littered with more profanity than Mumbai's roads are filled with potholes.

For, Salem's relationship with Bollywood was no one-way street. In addition to making his influence felt, he too was deeply influenced by Bollywood, its megalomania, its larger-than-life plots, its drama. He was fascinated by the idea of a dual identity.

He relished posing as Arsalan and would even go so far as to look at his cell phone every now and then and claim he had received a missed call from Salem bhai. He'd sometimes have imaginary conversations with this caller, even as the stars he was spending time with shuddered in fear.

Around this time, Salem had entered into a relationship with an attractive starlet who occupied the fringes of Bollywood. For a while, he used his second identity with her as well, before finally introducing himself as the dreaded Abu Salem. Taking advantage of her gullible nature, the gangster decided to put his moll to 'better use'. Salem's experience told him that the one common thing among producers, directors and actors was that they were all a bunch of liars. The starlet helped keep him in touch with these people's lives, their financial condition and their upcoming projects and so on.

The dreaded call from the Captain soon came to follow a set pattern. A typical scenario would entail the producer or director getting a call from the Captain. It's not hard to imagine the scene at the producer's end, the fumbling over the phone, the desperate search for ideas to outwit Salem.

'H-h-hello bhai,' the victim would manage to mumble.

Salem would make some small talk, just to break the ice. And then would ask if everything was all right.

'*Sab aapki kripa se, bhai,*' the hapless producer or director would reply, the ultimate choice of words for a desperate sycophant. And then, his tale of woe would begin.

'*Family mein death hui thi. Toh pichhle chaar–paanch hafton se koi kaam nahin kiya. Paisa bhi kam hai.*'

The call done, Salem would then ask his lady-on-the-inside to call the producer and check what was *actually* happening at his end. Salem's spy and lover would often come back with a contrasting report. While the producer had grovelled in front of Salem, he was back to playing a big shot as soon as he had finished the call. After getting the inside information on many such people, Salem would then respond with more threatening phone calls, warning his victim not to take him for a ride. Inevitably, they would succumb and pay up.

Salem got his lady friend to infiltrate the Bollywood network, even gaining access to the likes of Aamir Khan, J.P. Dutta and Rakesh Roshan. Whenever Salem received word that these people were about to disobey him or were unwilling to do his bidding, he'd send a subtle message like those sent to Ghai and Rai, and they'd fall right back in line. In short, the whole of Bollywood was now in Salem's back pocket.

Or so Salem thought.

TWELVE

CONSPIRACY IN DUBAI

12 June 1997

IT WAS PEGGED AS THE GLITZIEST party in all of Dubai, ever. Everyone who was anyone was going to be there. The entire Bollywood industry as well as all the movers and shakers of Mumbai and Dubai. Anis Ibrahim personally issued instructions to Abu Salem to round up Bollywood's top stars to show up at the party. After all, this was the launch of Vicky Goswami's Empire chain of hotels. Goswami, a notorious drug lord based in South Africa, whose friends and cronies included sheikhs, industrialists and assorted moneybags, was launching a chain of hotels across the world with the apparent objective of laundering some serious money.

Two of his most influential friends were Dawood and Anis Ibrahim.

When Salem first moved to Mumbai, film stars were citizens of an entirely different world from the one he inhabited. How things had changed in a matter of a few years—now this glittering galaxy of stars were constantly at his beck and call. The contrast between the way they were depicted interacting with people on-screen and the way they behaved with Salem was an unending source of amusement for him.

He wondered if the grovelling, weeping person on the other end of the line was really the same guy he saw beating up thirty people single-handedly or saving a school bus full of children and even catching a bullet with his bare hands on-screen, and with enough spare time to romance a pretty woman. Sometimes two.

Salem was briefed by Anis about this major bash. Anis explained in no uncertain terms that this was as big as it got and told Salem to ensure that Chunky Pandey, Jackie Shroff, Salman Khan, Shah Rukh Khan and the usual gaggle of names from the film fraternity were all present. Of course, no star-studded gala like this one would be considered even remotely complete without the women of Bollywood.

Goswami's parties were, in fact, not only always extremely lavish affairs but they were also attended by the most jaw-droppingly ravishing women. The sideshow activities would have once blown the mind of a young kid straight out of Pathan Tola in Sarai Mir village of Azamgarh. But Salem had been around the circuit long enough to have seen it all. This was nothing new to him. Coked-up, spaced out and sloshed starlets, who had previously never even tasted a sip of beer but nursed a burning desire to be seen at the 'right' parties were de rigueur at these soirées. Needless to say, these young women were always willing to dress in a manner that flaunted the advantages of a D-cup, and would gladly go the 'extra mile' for a role in a film or two.

Salem would initially gawk at these women who he had previously seen dancing gracefully on the big screen or playing an ideal housewife; they were now stumbling around in an intoxicated state, willing to go that 'extra mile'. But he got used to it soon enough.

Salem set about contacting everyone on his list. His intention was not to merely invite them to the party, but to inform them that if their personal health and safety was of any importance to them, then they would do well to attend the party. Who could argue with that? And so, hordes of actors and actresses descended upon Dubai. Tickets had been sent in advance. Now it was only a matter of picking each one up and bringing them to Royal Empire Hotel.

As expected, none of the stars had the impudence to ditch the party. It was a gala affair, with top stars having a whale of a time. Or at least giving the impression that they were enjoying themselves. The music was pumping, the liquor flowing and the food plentiful. Acres of smooth skin were on show, and heaving cleavages and slender waists cast a spell on the sheikhs and stars. A loud and drunken cheer went up as the state-of-the-art sound system emitted the opening strains of a song that had been topping the Hindi music charts for weeks.

Salem unfortunately was on duty that night. As he was taking care of the party, a glum-looking man approached him. It was the music composer Nadeem, part of the successful Nadeem–Shravan duo. Nadeem got straight to the point—which was to settle the matter of Gulshan. Nadeem's problems with music baron Gulshan Kumar were no secret. Wanting to keep matters as discreet as possible, Salem took Nadeem over to a corner and made him sit down comfortably and asked him if he wanted something to eat or drink. A shake of his head and a wave of his hand sent the waiter away and Nadeem began spilling the beans on his woes.

He related his tale of how Gulshan had made his life absolutely miserable and pleaded with Salem to find a solution to his problem. The more he spoke, the more agitated he became. Salem tried to convince him that things weren't as bad as he made them seem. After all, it was Gulshan who had given him and his partner Shravan Rathod their first big break by letting them compose the music for the 1990 Rahul Roy–Anu Agarwal starrer *Aashiqui*. But Nadeem was beyond reason. At one point, he stood up in anger and had to be taken by the arm and coerced gently back into his seat.

Salem told him that perhaps he would be able to help. A token payment of Rs 25 lakh from Nadeem would ensure that Gulshan would be 'taken care of'. Nadeem seemed relieved and went home from the party satisfied. Salem realized that while Nadeem may well have set the ball rolling, it would be himself who would stand to gain the most from this. If he caused the death of one of the brightest stars of the music industry, he would become one of the most feared members of the underworld.

For the next few days, Salem set about planning the final chapter of Gulshan Kumar's life. The shooter, the location, the time of day, escape routes and other such variables had to be charted out with total precision. Once he was totally satisfied with the plan, he would decide whether Gulshan should be given a hint of the doom that awaited him. If he wanted to play ball, Salem would allow him to pay up, but if he chose not to comply with Salem's diktat, then everything would have been planned already.

Meanwhile, Nadeem began to lose patience and got more desperate. He had already been told that the cost of 'dealing with' Gulshan was Rs 25 lakh. On 28 July 1997, at the Natural Ice Cream store in Juhu, Nadeem's men handed the amount in cold hard cash to three men sent by the gangster. Nadeem called Salem that evening and asked if he'd received the money. The music director implored the don again, the police would later claim.

Salem, on his part, said he would deliver on his end of the bargain, and then decided to fine-tune the big plan. He gathered all the information he could about Gulshan's daily routine. On 9 August, when everything was in place, Salem gave the T-Series chief a call and told him gently that he was working on Nadeem's behalf and had to protect his interests. And if he had any concern for his safety and well-being, Salem explained to Gulshan slowly, he would have to pay up.

Salem had expected the T-Series man to stand his ground for a little while and then eventually succumb to the demands as had other Bollywood supremos, Subhash Ghai and Rajiv Rai. Not once did he imagine that Gulshan would display outright defiance. He was incredulous that someone could think of opposing his will. The gangster told Gulshan that he would have to have him killed. The latter didn't seem to care. It hardly mattered to Salem. He had already decided that Gulshan's days were numbered.

THIRTEEN

AN EXECUTION, A WARNING

12 August 1997

THE DAY ETCHED FOREVER IN THE collective conscience of a city, the day music baron Gulshan Kumar breathed his last.

Gulshan Kumar began his working life as a fruit-juice vendor in Daryaganj in Delhi. After his Super Cassettes company in Noida turned hugely successful, he started T-Series, a label for Bollywood soundtracks and Hindu devotional songs. Salem had spent several months trying to convince the T-Series head honcho to cough up Rs 5 lakh a month. After all, the man had been donating crores of rupees annually to the Vaishno Devi temple and other religious institutions.

Salem instructed his subordinates to get their hands on Gulshan's daily and weekly schedules, so that he could study them. He wanted to know where Gulshan was at any given time of the day—when he ate, when he woke up and even when he visited the loo. He had to plan a foolproof hit on the music industry superstar.

After poring over his schedule, Salem discovered a window of opportunity before Gulshan headed off to work—when he would offer morning prayers at the Jeeteshwar Mahadev Mandir in Andheri. That was when they would strike. The location of the temple and the relief of its surroundings would give Salem's hitmen enough time to make a successful getaway. But that wasn't all. Salem had one more requirement—a perverse desire to hear Gulshan scream in agony and beg for his life as it was being taken from him.

And so, when the fateful day dawned, Salem's crack team took its positions near the temple. Salem actually believed that Gulshan knew they were coming for him. Perhaps it was Gulshan's undying faith that led him to believe that God would not let one of his children die at the hands of someone like Salem. Anyway, he had decided not to approach the police, come what may.

The only precaution Gulshan had taken was in hiring a personal security guard. The security guard was known to be rather irregular and had decided for the second day in a row that he would not turn up. It takes a person of rare conviction to take a risk and not to give the temple a miss. Gulshan's single-minded devotion was one of the things Salem counted on when hatching his plan. Once the security guard was out of the way, there seemed to be little doubt—in Salem's mind anyway—that his shooters would be successful.

Undaunted, Gulshan went alone to the temple, and a few minutes after 10 a.m., Salem's phone began to ring. One of his hitmen, a man named Raja, was calling so that his boss could get a 'ringside view' of the killing. *'Bhai, woh mandir se nikal gaya,'* said the caller and left the call active so that Salem could listen to every scream.

Glued to his phone, Salem listened carefully to his hired gun's footsteps as he followed the music producer. His footsteps made a distinctive clacking sound against the asphalt road as he followed Gulshan's comparatively slower and more muted steps. Salem could hear the sound of the slight breeze through the cell phone, some birds chirping overhead and the faint sounds of people's voices. Then the first shot rang out, shattering the serenity of the moment.

Raja kept silent throughout. Presumably, he did not want to displease his boss by causing him to miss so much as a single decibel. Salem couldn't tell where Gulshan had been hit, but he could hear his muffled howls of pain. Almost immediately, Salem heard a distant sound of the shuffle of slippers against asphalt, sounds of heavy feet dragging along the ground a little quicker than before. Gulshan was on the run.

The steady rhythm of Raja's assured and calm footsteps signified to Salem that he did not run after Gulshan. Instead, he was like a true predator—stalking his prey, waiting patiently, sizing him up and savouring the moments before making the kill. It is believed that at this point, Gulshan tried to take cover and hide in a public toilet. Unfortunately, he slipped on his way inside, thereby alerting Raja. As the assassin followed him in, the footsteps began echoing and Salem could tell that the killer and his prey were indoors. Unsurprisingly, bystanders chose to stand by rather than interfere. All of Gulshan's charitable acts were forgotten in that instant.

It was only a matter of seconds before Raja pulled the trigger again and another shot rang out, resulting in another scream from Gulshan. The macabre and theatrical execution was slowly winding down and was about to reach its bloody conclusion. Gulshan had been hit and had fallen down. He whimpered and groaned in pain, but true to his indomitable spirit continued to battle the odds, trying to crawl away. Raja walked calmly towards Gulshan and discharged another round.

Raja would later tell Salem that he could see the white-hot fear in Gulshan's eyes as he stalked him. To his credit, Gulshan managed to drag himself out of the toilet and make a beeline for the neighbouring slum area.

Raja walked slowly after him. The T-Series supremo was requesting people to give him refuge or at least hide him temporarily. They didn't. It was to be a tragic end for a man who was a great philanthropist.

Salem then heard Gulshan asking an old woman to let him into her hut. He realized it had been around ten to fifteen minutes since the execution had begun. He issued instructions to Raja to wrap it up and get out of there. Raja approached Gulshan, who begged Raja to spare him. And Salem finally got to hear what he had been aching to hear for so long—the sound of the once-defiant music mogul begging for mercy. Raja pumped six rounds into Gulshan and left him for dead as he rode off on his bike.

India was shocked. Mumbai had witnessed many mafia killings, but this one surpassed everything. Salem's monstrosity was discussed from Parliament to pub houses. The prime minister of the coalition government, Inder Kumar Gujral, reacted immediately to the killing: 'This criminal act is totally out of place in a civilized society and particularly in a city known for its discipline and civic consciousness. Gulshan Kumar,' Gujral said, had 'carved a niche for himself in the world of film music. His loss will be mourned by all music-loving people.' Headlines screamed Salem's name and asked for justice. The furore felt like accolades to Salem. He was delighted that the *Times of India* and the *Indian Express* had branded him L'Enfant Terrible of the Underworld.

The film fraternity froze with fear at the murder. Director Mahesh Bhatt, who directed the hit *Aashiqui*—which featured music produced by T-Series—summed it up aptly when he said, 'When you kill Gulshan Kumar, you kill one of the biggest people in the entertainment industry. By killing Gulshan Kumar they are saying, "We are calling the shots," and they have proved it . . . The entire film fraternity is in a state of terror.'

FOURTEEN

EXTRADITION EMBARRASSMENT

SALEM WAS DETAINED IN DUBAI CENTRAL Jail at Al Aweer Road, within a week of Gulshan Kumar's murder. Less than a month later, at a strategically planned police conference, the new police commissioner R.H. Mendonca named musician Nadeem Saifi as a prime suspect in the killing.

The mention of Nadeem's name at the packed-to-the-rafters press conference sent shockwaves through the country. It was almost as shocking as the disclosure of film star Sanjay Dutt's purchase of weapons during Mumbai's serial blasts. The skeletons had begun tumbling out of Bollywood's tightly locked cupboard.

Like Sanjay, Nadeem too belonged to a highly respectable family. His father Yunus Saifi was the largest publisher and distributor of the Holy Quran in the country. The Taj Book House, right across Mumbai's famous Minara Masjid at Mohammad Ali Road in the Muslim segment of South Mumbai, is regarded as the hub for Islamic book lovers across the Indian peninsula.

Saifi Senior, a devout Muslim, was shattered at the allegations. 'We belong to a scrupulous family. My son has been brought up on the sublime ideals of the Quran. He will never kill or be part of any killing,' he said, tears streaming down his cheeks. Nadeem, who was based in London, was also rattled at the developments in Mumbai. He immediately called Mendonca and assured him that there had been some sort of a mistake. He promised to take the first flight into Mumbai and cooperate with the investigation. 'Gulshanji was like my father. I cannot even imagine killing him,' Nadeem reportedly told the top cop on the phone.

The government, however, was in no mood to buy Nadeem's explanations. It was by now in a tearing hurry to indict him and bring him to India, with or without his cooperation. On 4 September, the Mumbai Police formally approached Interpol seeking his arrest and on 17 September, Nadeem received a call from the Metropolitan Police asking him to present himself at the Charring Cross police station.

Nadeem gave himself up at the station, accompanied by his solicitor, Henry Bradman. He was charged with conspiracy to murder. Subsequently, the extradition department of the New Scotland Yard took over and he was produced at the Bow Street Magistrate's Court in Covent Garden. Bail for Nadeem was set by Magistrate Ronald Bartle at GBP 200,000 in financial guarantees, and his passport was confiscated, to prevent him from fleeing the country.

Nadeem was also instructed not to leave his Kingsbury address until the next court hearing on 24 September. Kingsbury, a posh suburb in Middlesex, is home to many corporate executives, bankers and mid-level businessman. Over the years, it had become a neighbourhood populated by Asian expatriates, especially Gujaratis and other nouveau riche Indians. Kingsbury, like neighbouring Harrow, represented the affluence of the Indian diaspora in and around London. Nadeem's wife Sultana had suffered a miscarriage after five months of pregnancy, which led to Nadeem's decision not to return to India. The Mumbai Police could only get him if they managed to extradite him from the UK.

There was now a long legal battle on the cards for the music composer and the Mumbai Police. The crown prosecution service would ask the Mumbai Police to present evidence against Nadeem, on the basis of which a decision on extradition would be taken. When reporters began investigating why the government had been so quick in indicting Nadeem and seeking an Interpol notice against him, Maharashtra Deputy Chief Minister and Home Minister Gopinath Munde explained, 'We wanted to extradite him because it's easier to get him from London than Dubai. Were he to go to Dubai, it would be impossible to bring him back.'

Munde must have forgotten that India had consistently failed to get its accused back from Britain. One prominent instance was that of Iqbal Mohammad Memon (aka Iqbal Mirchi). The Maharashtra state government which spent an obscene amount of money in court proceedings in both cases not only faced abysmal failure but even ended up paying costs and damages to both the accused in foreign currency.

Mirchi, who had been on the lam ever since his escape from India in the early 1990s, was arrested from his home in England by the Scotland Yard in April 1995 and charged with possession of drugs. With two drug cases pending against Mirchi in Mumbai courts (in 1986 and 1994), the legal team sought to have him extradited and brought back to the city of his birth, where he would be tried. Everything seemed to be in order and extradition seemed all but imminent. Except for one tiny glitch. According to the extradition treaty drawn up between India and the United Kingdom, all the documents upon which the case was based had to be authenticated by the minister of state for external affairs.

As it turned out, in a huge gaffe that nobody could explain, the entire charge sheet against Mirchi was authenticated by some other official, not the minister of state for external affairs. As a result, no material could be put before the British authorities. And the extradition request was turned down by the Bow Street magistrates. India did not even appeal the decision.

Mirchi's case had gone on for just four brief months. Nobody from the CBI or any other investigating agency, government office or the Indian police had even gone to London for it. An officer from the Indian High Commission was the only representative of the Indian government at the hearings. Advocate Ram Jethmalani, who had gone to London to argue the case against Mirchi, recounts that the main point raised by the British counsel was: 'Where is the authentication from the Indian government?' There was, apparently, no answer to that question.

India, inexplicably, made the same blunder in the Nadeem case. The Government of India had sought the extradition of Nadeem. This time around, Public Prosecutor Ujjwal Nikam and advocate Majeed Memon went to London. But they needn't have bothered. The case ran its course for three to four months and was dismissed. The reason? A lack of authentication by the minister of state for external affairs!

In retrospect, and in Jethmalani's view, it never seemed like the Indian government was keen on having either of the two extradited. 'The Government of India has its own priorities that do not include bringing back accused who have been arrested overseas. There has been absolutely zero application of mind and the government has for some reason or other been disinterested in bringing the duo back to India,' he said.

The cops maintained that they had evidence against Nadeem. When his non-film album *Hi Ajnabi* failed, he had squarely blamed Gulshan Kumar. 'Have you received calls from my friends? You don't know me,' Nadeem reportedly threatened Gulshan. Apart from family statements and other indications about the growing acrimony between Gulshan Kumar and Nadeem, the biggest evidence that the cops banked on was the statement of several film stars who were present at the opening of the Royal Empire Hotel on 12 June, where the Nadeem–Shravan duo had performed for free, allegedly at the behest of Salem.

Film stars, including Shah Rukh Khan, Salman Khan, Jackie Shroff, Aditya Pancholi, Atul Agnihotri, Chunky Pandey and Pooja Bhatt, were summoned to the Crime Branch for their statements to be recorded. The police claimed that they had managed to piece together evidence from their statements and corroborated how

Nadeem was sitting with Salem for hours and hatching the plan to take out Gulshan if he failed to agree to the terms set by Nadeem.

Unlike the way the film industry folks and others rallied behind Sanjay Dutt—including his father's political detractors, Shatrughan Sinha and Bal Thackeray—when he was arrested, Nadeem had no supporters. His repeated pleas seeking intervention from Thackeray, whom he kept referring to as 'Thackeray Uncle', did not work in his favour either. Like Mirchi, who never returned to Indian shores, Nadeem, too, was destined to remain holed up in London.

FIFTEEN

THE FALLOUT

EVER SINCE SALEM ARRIVED IN DUBAI, he had been filling Anis's dwindling coffers. In fact, Salem was Anis's most loyal soldier, but the latter did not reciprocate equally. When the noose tightened around Salem's neck, his boss did not stand up for him. Gulshan Kumar's killing had appalled the Indian government and they had used diplomatic channels to put pressure on the UAE government to hand Salem over.

The signing of an extradition treaty in 1996 between the UAE and Indian governments had been a landmark event. The treaty bolstered the Mumbai Police's efforts in launching an offensive against organized crime. They had failed to extradite Dawood following the serial blasts, because such a treaty did not exist in 1994. But this time they were confident that they would not allow Salem to slip through their fingers.

The Dubai government, upon checking records of Indians living under the residential visa programme, found no one by the name of Abu Salem Ansari in Dubai. The Dubai government's response unsettled the Indian bureaucrats and police. However, the CBI, the nodal agency for the Mumbai Police to deal with foreign police and governments, refused to give up easily. They swung into action with renewed vigour and got several agencies working in tandem.

This time they managed to dig out details on Salem, including his criminal profile, his photographs and his fingerprints from D.N. Nagar police station and sent a detailed dossier to the Dubai government. The Dubai Shurta, or CID, realized that these details matched a Deira resident, Akil Ahmed Azmi, whose passport had been issued from Lucknow.

As soon as this development came to light, Azmi (i.e. Salem) was detained in Dubai and thrown behind bars along with ordinary criminals. Salem was shocked at the treatment meted out to him. He was being treated like an ordinary criminal, something that had not happened to him even in Azamgarh or Mumbai, barring a couple of days at the D.N. Nagar police station.

Salem had witnessed the power of Dawood's connections in the past. He was capable of having anyone released or locked away for all eternity, depending on how he felt. Salem's grouse was that if Anis had wanted, he could have had him released from police custody in no time.

In 1995, for example, when Sunil Sawant, one of Dawood's sharpshooters, was killed in Dubai by Chhota Rajan's contract killers, the local police had detained Sharad Shetty, the kingpin of the cricket betting racket, and Anil Parab, alias Wangya, Dawood's one-time sharpshooter. Shetty had managed to convince Dawood that he was innocent, while Wangya could not. Dawood ensured that Shetty was released within hours of his detention, while Wangya had to suffer incarceration for three months, with no help from the Company.

Days passed and Salem kept expecting help from his bosses, but it never came. Days turned into weeks and the weeks melted into months, but there was no sign of any reprieve for Salem. He was rotting in jail, along with ordinary pickpockets and petty thieves, and no one tried to get him out. Worse, Salem learnt, his wife Sameera had been left to fend for herself with nobody offering her financial assistance or even visiting her. Sameera had left her family behind to marry Salem and now she was alone in an alien city without a shoulder to lean on. She also had to coordinate with lawyers, meet Salem in jail, and follow his instructions about collection and distribution of finances.

Even the slightest support from the Company would have lifted Sameera's morale. Salem had imagined that the blood, sweat and tears he had expended on the Company would earn him and his wife assistance in their hour of need. But Anis turned out to be a fair-weather friend. Not once did he visit or provide assurances of expediting Salem's release. The once-dreaded scourge of Mumbai was alone and abandoned.

In the meantime, the efforts of the Indian government to extradite Salem had begun losing steam. The Dubai courts went on to rule against the extradition of Akil Ahmed Azmi of Lucknow. The Indian government was left shell-shocked.

Salem returned to his house in Dubai a transformed man. He looked back at his empire. From a life of poverty, he had built a vast fortune and in the process, had lined Anis's pockets too. Anis had been happy to reap the fruits of Salem's handiwork, but when it came to reciprocate and be a good boss, he had ignored Salem. What irked Salem the most was being treated by Anis as no more than a glorified errand boy.

He was never treated with civility in the presence of other Company members. Sometimes, Anis deliberately humiliated him by chiding him for no reason in front of others or made him do a small task when he could have asked any of his several servants instead. But Salem quietly swallowed his pride and remained subservient to

Anis. But the period in jail had taught him one thing—Anis was not someone who could be relied on in a crisis.

His frustration began to grow, and he now started to spend more time with his friends and lackeys; he also threw himself into philandering with starlets flocking to visit him in Dubai. His marriage, which had never been happy since Dubai, now began to crack. Sameera was an outspoken woman with a bitter, sharp tongue when she was angry. Salem found it hard to tolerate her anger and blunt remarks, and began to beat her up regularly. He once hit her so hard that she had a deep gash on her forehead. She was rushed to a hospital bleeding profusely and was sent home with twelve stitches.

Salem also lost interest in his work. He was not keen on making any more money for Anis and, as a result, stopped making calls to India. The extortion business came to a standstill. He suddenly stopped going to his office. The Indian business community and Bollywood breathed a sigh of relief.

Eventually, Salem decided to go his own way, knowing that he did not need Anis as much as Anis needed him. As a first step, he pulled down the huge portrait of Anis that adorned his office wall. Then, in a fit of anger, he smashed the frame and tore the portrait.

News of Salem's intentions could not have been kept away from Anis. Losing no time, Anis landed up at Salem's house at Jumeirah. When he did not find

Salem, he screamed at Sameera and spoke to her rather rudely, leaving her rattled. She was probably the only educated woman in the entire fraternity and did not hesitate to convey her disgust to Dawood through Chhota Shakeel's wife. Dawood called her up to inquire about what had happened. When Sameera complained to him about his younger brother's behaviour, Dawood sounded apologetic and assured her that she would not be bothered any more.

Dawood had by then relocated to Karachi, but made a trip to Dubai to mediate between Anis and Salem so that they could be friends again. Both Anis and Salem respected Dawood immensely and there was no way either of them could refuse him. They agreed to a truce, but there was an underlying tension now in their friendship. While Anis had begun to dislike Salem, the latter had lost all respect for his one-time boss and mentor.

Salem knew too that with the hounds of the Indian government hot on his trail, it was possible that he could get into trouble again. He had to protect himself and Sameera. It was circa 1998 and he slowly began planning to leave Dubai and settle down elsewhere. It would not happen overnight. It would require a lot of planning, transferring of funds, getting a house elsewhere and investing in some properties abroad.

Salem decided to first shift Sameera so that Anis could

not torment her any longer. He would join her later. He began weighing his options. Pakistan, already a safe haven for thirty-three of the accused in the serial blasts and other gangsters, was ruled out. Dawood would have been happy to have him there and Salem had been to Karachi once during Dawood's brother Mustaqim's wedding; but there was no way Anis would allow him to rest in peace there. No country in the Gulf would be safe for him either.

After much thinking, Salem decided that the USA would be the best bet. Anis would not be able to touch him there. He zeroed in on Atlanta, Georgia. But Sameera would need a new identity before she could leave. Salem needed to procure a fresh set of passports for both of them. Salem got in touch with his contacts in Hyderabad for new identities and passports.

SIXTEEN

DUGGAL'S DOLL

MONICA BEDI WAS BORN TO A middle-class Sikh family in a small village in Chabbewal, fifteen kilometres from the town of Hoshiarpur in Punjab, on 18 January 1975. Her father Prem Bedi was a doctor, while mother Shakuntala was a housewife. It was an era when most Punjabi families aspired to migrate to the West in search of their fortunes. Even before Monica's first birthday, Dr Bedi had decided to move his family to Norway.

In the 1970s, the Indian diaspora in Norway comprised a few hundred or so people, and lived as a close-knit community. Upon arriving in his new country, Dr Bedi quit his medical practice and launched his own garment business in the city of Drammen, forty-five kilometres from Norway's capital, Oslo. Dr

Bedi pampered his daughter Monica and son Bobby. The siblings grew up on a heavy dose of Bollywood through video cassettes of Hindi films—perhaps their only connect with their country and people back home.

In 1992, at the age of seventeen, Monica moved to the UK to study English literature at Oxford University. Initially, her parents protested as they had given her a sheltered upbringing. But she wanted to live life on her own terms. London was beautiful. Monica grew in those years into a strong-willed woman. But she got tired of her studies soon and yearned to give up the course. Giving up her studies meant losing her ticket to freedom. But one holiday to Mumbai turned her life around.

In Mumbai, Monica enrolled herself at the Gopi Kishan Dance Classes to learn Kathak. One day, film icon Manoj Kumar dropped by on a personal errand. As a child, Monica had watched Manoj Kumar in *Roti Kapda Aur Makaan* and *Upkaar*. He had aged since, but his charm and star quality were still intact. Manoj Kumar reportedly said to Monica that her face was the perfect blend of the actresses of the 1950s and 1960s and the novelty needed for Indian cinema today.

This sparked the young woman's ambitions. She was turning eighteen, had a flawless complexion, an attractive figure, a seductive smile and, at a height of five feet five inches, she had all the qualities needed to be a star. Monica also later claimed that Manoj Kumar wanted to launch her in a movie with his son Kunal.

She immediately called her parents and told them that she wanted to try her luck in the film industry. They tried to dissuade her, telling her that Bollywood was notorious for exploiting women and no place for a cultured young woman like her. But Monica had now seen her future in films and no one could stop her from giving it a shot.

When the parents realized that they would not be able to convince their obstinate daughter, Shakuntala decided to shift base to Mumbai. Monica had her portfolio made and took the plunge. She had heard that there were two ways to achieve success in the world of cinema—either she would have to sleep her way through to major contracts or attend a lot of film events and draw the attention of the movie moguls. Monica later said in her interviews that she decided to attend Bollywood parties and events to get noticed.

One of the parties she would attend was Subhash Ghai's famous Holi get-together. Monica later claimed that she got lucky as she bumped into Rakesh Roshan during the celebrations. She had seen some of his films in her childhood and was surprised to hear that he was launching a film—*Karan Arjun*—and needed a fresh face opposite Salman Khan. He insisted that she visit him at his Santa Cruz office as he was considering casting her in the role.

Roshan also gave her his office address and phone number, but Monica, sceptical of his intentions, did not turn up for the audition. She thought that he was an old-time actor and wondered how he could launch her in the movies. Monica would later admit that she had no clue Rakesh Roshan was already a successful film-maker. In any case, she never contacted him again. The role eventually went to Mamta Kulkarni and the film went on to become the second highest grossing film of 1995 after *Dilwale Dulhaniya Le Jaayenge*. Monica's snub would prove to be one of the costliest blunders of her career. Months passed and Monica had no film offers.

In the meantime, bandits attacked her family in Chabbewal and brutally killed her grandparents. This left her mother devastated, forcing her to return to Norway. Alone in Mumbai, Monica was now in a do-or-die situation. Casting aside her pride, she decided to go out seeking work. This was how she met the controversial film-maker Mukesh Duggal who launched her in his film *Suraksha*. Despite a decent star cast of Saif Ali Khan and Suniel Shetty, the film tanked at the box office and with it, Monica's dreams.

But Duggal did not give up on Monica. He tried to promote her in a big way and continued to give her bit roles in his films. Their frequent collaborations fuelled rumours of an affair and Monica was labelled as 'Duggal's darling', a tag she detested but could do little about. The director was widely known for his links to the underworld and of being especially close to Abu Salem. On one of his trips to Dubai with Monica, he introduced her to Salem.

Monica explained later that she was introduced to 'Arsalan Ali', a Pakistani event manager based in Dubai, who organized shows for Bollywood personalities across the globe. It is possible, given her ignorance of Rakesh Roshan's stature as a film-maker, that she did not know that Salem was a gangster.

Monica and 'Arsalan' had an immediate connection and began talking to each other regularly. Soon, Monica began to look forward to his calls every day. She realized that although she spoke to him in English, the suave-looking man could not say very much more than 'hello' and 'thank you'. After befriending Arsalan, Monica began receiving roles in some Telugu films. She had no idea that Salem was behind these. However, despite his 'help', she was unable to make a mark in the industry.

Then came another tragedy. In March 1997, Mukesh Duggal was shot dead by two gunmen outside his office in Andheri. Duggal was shot dead by Chhota Shakeel's sharpshooters because Shakeel believed that the film-maker was his rival Chhota Rajan's supporter and was laundering his money by making films. Shakeel had said so in an interview to the *Indian Express* on the night of the killing. But it later surfaced that Shakeel regretted killing Duggal—he was not aware of the late director's friendship with Salem. Had Shakeel known that Duggal was a friend of the Company's, he would have still been alive.

With Duggal's death, Monica had no godfather in the industry any more. Arsalan assured her that he would use his contacts in the film world. Monica did not take him seriously. But to her surprise, a host of B-grade film-makers and little-known producers started to make a beeline to sign Monica Bedi in their movies. It was almost a dream come true.

Her films in this period included *Ek Phool Teen Kaante*, *Tirchhi Topiwale*, *Mera Desh*, *Kalicharan*, *Zanjeer*, *Loh Purush* and *Kaala Samrajya*. However, none of them made a splash at the box office, earning her the unfortunate description of a 'heroine of B-grade movies'. Monica was confused about her lack of success, and blamed a hostile media. But she did not lose heart. Arsalan kept encouraging her, but she needed a stronger push, a bigger break, more prestigious banners, and interest from top directors or production houses. Monica was unhappy with mere survival—she wanted success at any cost.

SEVENTEEN

THE DON'S DARLING

MONICA'S INNOCENCE HAD CAPTIVATED SALEM'S HEART. Never before had he felt such a burning desire to help someone. Monica began making frequent trips to Dubai. She would meet him every day she was there, spending most of her time with him. Even when she was not in Dubai, Monica would call him frequently. Salem was drifting further and further away from Sameera and was being increasingly drawn to Monica's charms. He still hadn't told Monica about his true identity, worried as he was that it would drive her away.

Men are peculiar animals. They never take responsibility for their infidelity and look for any justification to cheat. Salem was especially good at this. When he was having his many brief affairs or one-night stands with starlets, he rationalized that it was because they were far too beautiful to resist or that they had seduced him. He never saw himself as the seducer.

When he fell in love with Monica, Salem came up with a totally different set of explanations. Sameera had distanced herself from him, he told himself. He needed someone to understand him and support him, and it was in Monica that he found this support. Those familiar with Salem's ways knew that this was just another way of fooling Sameera, to justify his latest fling to his own conscience. But it was serious enough for Salem to begin contemplating divorce.

For Sameera, Monica was no different from all those starlets who caught Salem's fancy for a few weeks. She had always maintained a stoic silence about Salem's infidelities, understanding that loyalty was a virtue not known to him. Sameera thus never felt threatened by Monica or by Salem's increasing fondness for her. However, she decided to make one last effort to save her marriage. No family is complete without a child and she wondered if perhaps her husband too harboured an unspoken desire for one. Perhaps a child would rekindle their romance.

If in every marriage it is the woman who makes the most sacrifices and takes the most risks, in Sameera's case this was doubly so. She had left her religion, her parents and her city for an outlaw of a husband who had no conception of fidelity. Sameera decided to make one more sacrifice and give the marriage another shot.

Sadly, Sameera's plan backfired. She went through her pregnancy on her own. Salem was never by her side and was completely oblivious towards her or her needs. When Sameera was eight months' pregnant, she travelled to New Jersey, where her aunt lived, to deliver her child. She knew that she could not count on her husband for emotional support during the delivery. Returning to Mumbai was ruled out as she had been in the police's wanted list since 1993. America seemed to be the safest place and it was also the country where Salem was trying to get a house for Sameera. On 30 August 1997, Sameera gave birth to a boy. He was named Amir. What hurt the new mother most was that Salem did not even take the trouble to travel to New Jersey to see his baby. Salem was too wrapped up in himself and in his growing relationship with Monica.

Salem's new relationship had another by-product—narcissism. He had always been vain and boastful. He considered himself very good-looking and loved attention of all kind. He was even derisively referred to as Paper Don in Dubai because he used to procure Indian newspapers that mentioned his name in the headlines, and would save the clippings. Later, Salem even admitted to the sleuths from the CBI that he had claimed credit for a lot of killings in Mumbai in which he was actually not involved.

Now he became obsessed with his looks, spending hours looking at and examining himself—his skin, the crow's feet under his eyes, his nose and so on. His nose, he had always felt, was imperfect, and he went under the knife and got himself a more angular nose. Salem also grew fond of manicures and pedicures, and his dressing table groaned under the weight of anti-ageing creams, skin lotions, herbal potions and other cosmetics. He began spending hours at the gym and even more in front of the mirror. Even when he was threatening his victims on the phone, he would check his reflection.

Monica also cultivated his interest in branded clothes, sunglasses and shoes, and under her tutelage, Salem began to look slicker than he ever had. Soon, Salem was heard boasting to his friends that he was no less handsome than Salman Khan. He would claim that in different circumstances, he would have been competing with Salman in Bollywood as a leading man. People would smile at his delusional self-obsession, suspecting that it was Monica who had put such thoughts into his head.

In any case, Salem was genuinely happy with Monica's arrival in his life. His bosses and aides saw him fawning over her, including Anis who had still not got over his anger towards Salem. He decided to test the waters now and instructed Salem to send Monica over to him for a night. Anis knew that Salem's relationship with Monica was hardly like that with other girls. She was the love of his life. Salem didn't see her as a regular packet of chips to be passed around among friends. When Anis told Salem, *'Kya item hai! Aaj raat mere paas bhej de,'* he broke his protégé's heart.

That was the final straw. Salem realized he could not work with this man any more. After everything he had done for Anis and all the efforts to please him despite the stiff competition from Shakeel, this really stung. It was time to make a clean break. As Salem put the finishing touches to his getaway, he made one alteration to his plan. While making a fake passport for himself and Sameera, he also organized for a second passport for Monica.

The plan was to send wife and son ahead of him. Salem would take care of pending business in Dubai and join them. Sameera's passport—ordered from Hyderabad—bore the name of Neha Asif Jafri, while his own passport had the distinctly different name of Ramil Kamil Malik. And, since he wanted to travel with Monica in tow, he got a similar-sounding name on her passport, Sana Kamil Malik. It only seemed apt that the wife's name be similar to her husband's.

Salem may have got several fake passports for Sameera, but she never used any of them. She travelled to the US on the same Indian passport of Sabina Azmi, which had been issued from Lucknow and which she had used for escaping from Delhi to join Salem in Dubai in 1993. Sameera arrived in Gwinnett County in Georgia in September 1999 and moved to a house that Salem had bought for her. In Georgia, she was known as Sabina Azmi, the wife of Akil Azmi. Her son was called Amir Azmi. Finally, she thought she had a chance to start her life afresh.

EIGHTEEN

A STARLET'S RISE

MAFIA DONS ARE, BY AND LARGE, more partial to one-night stands and brief affairs, hardly ever entertaining the thought of a serious relationship. But Salem ventured into forbidden territory with Monica. Everyone around Salem was taken by surprise at this development, most of all Salem himself.

He had bedded some of the most ravishing sirens from the film industry, including a major beauty queen. But Monica was different. She had neither won crowns at beauty pageants, nor was she a contender for top billing in films. But there was something irresistible about her. Something he had not seen in the 'plastic' divas of the film world.

Salem wanted to marry her and take her with him

to the USA. But before that, he wanted to ensure that Monica reached the top league of Indian actresses. He felt that once she became a successful actress, she would be beholden to Salem and would not refuse a marriage proposal. It's impossible to know for sure how many people got calls from Salem and which of them agreed to his demands, but Monica did get her first big break—the sort she had been waiting for all her life.

The film was called *Jaanam Samjha Karo*, scripted by Rajkumar Santoshi and directed by Andaleeb Sultanpuri, and released in April 1999. It had a star cast of big hitters like Salman Khan and Urmila Matondkar. Although Monica was touted as the second lead in the film and paired with Salman, she had only a minuscule role. It seemed quite evident that she was cast in a blink-and-miss appearance only to appease Salem and ward off his menacing calls.

But Monica got what she wanted—an ascent from seedy banners and B-grade actors to sharing screen time with none other than Salman Khan. She was certain that this would perk up her future prospects. But Salem was disappointed with the movie and with Monica's role in it. He knew the job of turning Monica into a star was far from over.

The next big project that he landed for Monica was *Jodi No. 1*, directed by David Dhawan, with such top-line actors as Sanjay Dutt, Govinda and Twinkle

Khanna. Ironically, Monica was paired with Sanjay, who had been given preferential billing over Govinda. However, Sanjay is believed to have been very upset with the casting of his romantic interest. He protested that if Govinda could get a top star like Twinkle, how come he was asked to work with a B-grade starlet like Monica Bedi? He considered quitting the movie, but one phone call made him change his mind.

Sanjay was told in no uncertain terms that he had no option but to work with Monica and he was expected to be respectful to her—so much so that he was not even to hold her too firmly during the romantic scenes. Salem's spine-chilling ultimatum was enough to make everyone on the sets wary. The result was that throughout the movie, Sanjay and Monica did not so much as gaze at each other lovingly, let alone display any physical chemistry. Sanjay was no longer working with Monica the actress; he was working with Monica, his *bhabhi*. The movie did average business on the strength of the comical pair of Sanjay–Govinda and because of Dhawan's standing in the market.

But for Monica, things had started looking up. She was being treated with respect and everyone wanted to please her. She had started enjoying her newfound respect, and basked in its glory. She was that much closer to being the superhit actress she had always dreamed of becoming.

Soon, Salem managed to get through to Rajiv Rai, one of the most respected directors in the industry, and forced him to sign Monica on for his next film. Rai had produced hits such as *Tridev* with Sunny Deol, Naseeruddin Shah, Madhuri Dixit and Jackie Shroff, and *Mohra* with Akshay Kumar and Suniel Shetty. Widely considered to be a big name in the industry, Rai was in the process of making *Pyar Ishq Mohabbat* with Kirti Reddy, Suniel Shetty and Arjun Rampal.

There was no scope for another leading lady. But Salem had threatened Rai once in July 1997 and he knew that he had succeeded in frightening him. There was no way that Rai would refuse his 'polite suggestion'. Rai buckled under the pressure and brought her into the film, but completely lost interest in the project. Released in September 2001, *Pyar Ishq Mohabbat* was a box office disaster and Rai lost a considerable amount of money on it. Since Monica did not have a substantial role in the film, Rai feared a backlash from Salem and thought it best to leave the city.

Meanwhile, the media had got wind of Monica getting roles as a result of her association with Abu Salem. Journalists began investigating the threats received by the film-makers. The producers of *Jodi No. 1* denied any duress in casting Monica and so did Rai. But the stories had begun appearing in the newspapers. Rai immediately shifted base and migrated to America.

Rai's migration to the US shook the industry, and Salem's growing menace now forced them into action. They decided to approach the government and make a case for their safety. For the state government, it had also become a prestige issue as the business community had begun showing a lack of faith in the security system and preferred to move to some other city.

In the meantime, Salem had begun facing problems everywhere. The hordes of enemies he had made were baying for his blood. Anis had heard about his sly plans to relocate, so he had begun making plans to snitch on him to the Dubai government or to the CBI officers, while Shakeel was waiting to bump him off at the first available opportunity. His other detractors in the Company had also begun their backbiting. The CBI and IB had stepped up their efforts to extradite him and monitored each of his moves. Salem felt as if his enemies were closing in on him.

Salem asked Monica to leave Mumbai at once and head to Dubai. She was not prepared for this abrupt departure, particularly since her career had just shown signs of improving. After much back and forth, Salem finally dropped the bombshell: It was a choice between either leaving now for safer shores or spending her life in jail. Salem had discovered that Monica was increasingly attracting the suspicion of the police. They were just waiting for any evidence to tighten the noose around her, charging her of being complicit with Salem. This was enough for Monica. She decided that she would rather flee. With a heavy heart, she left tinsel town, her dreams of stardom cruelly crushed.

NINETEEN

SALEM IN SOUTH AFRICA

IN OCTOBER 1999, THE TWO LEFT Dubai for good. Salem did not want Anis to get wind of his plans to escape, for he could rat him out to the CBI. Salem was a proclaimed offender and an accused in the serial blasts case, and would most certainly be arrested overseas if found out. He needed to sneak out of Dubai stealthily, a thief decamping after emptying a rich man's locker.

From his experience in Mumbai in the days following the serial blasts, Salem knew that a good plan to escape from the law enforcers was always the one in which it is completely impossible to predict in which direction the trail will turn. After getting forged passports prepared in Hyderabad, Salem got another set of forged passports made in Bhopal. His own passport bore the name Danish

Beg while Sameera's was Rubina Beg. Monica would travel under the name Fauzia Usman. The idea behind a stack of different identities was to ensure that they were always prepared to become someone else in an hour of sudden need.

And it was through this method that Salem and Monica embarked on their world tour, partly out of desperation, partly for pleasure. Salem was trying to hunt for a safe location that could double up as his new base. At the same time, he wanted to ensure that Anis Ibrahim's hounds could not locate him. He also wanted a king-size life. That was always very important to Salem. He wanted to drive the finest cars, dine at the finest restaurants, live in the finest house, bathe in the finest bathroom and make love on the finest bed money could buy.

In his search for a new hideout, Asia was a total no-go zone. The Middle East and Pakistan was D-Company territory. By association, Bangladesh, Sri Lanka and Nepal were all out of the question. As for South East Asia, Cambodia was Chhota Rajan's HQ and going anywhere near there would be foolish. The Rainbow Nation would be their first choice.

Salem had never been to Africa, so the journey had an air of infectious uncertainty and excitement to it. Monica seemed excited too about visiting a new country. They travelled extensively around Johannesburg and

Cape Town. Salem was fascinated that these two cities seemed so modern and advanced on the one hand and yet had the kind of poverty that reminded him of home. Over time, the fugitive gangster spread his wings and travelled all across Africa, spending some time in the Kenyan capital of Nairobi as well.

But, having travelled up and down the continent for six long months, they couldn't decide on a place to settle down. The cities they visited all had their own charms, but there was always one problem or the other. If they didn't really blend in too well with the local Indian crowds, then they couldn't find a home that matched Salem's lofty standards. In other places, the locals recognized Monica and, in doing so, blew their cover. Half a year later, the safari was over and it was time to search for a new continent to set up camp in.

In the meantime, Salem was counting the months since he had last earned any money. The last lucrative days had been in Dubai. He was getting increasingly concerned about his dwindling finances when, out of the blue, came a windfall that not only stabilized his money situation, but also taught him a few lessons in life. In the decade and a half he had spent in crime, Salem felt he had seen everything. But this treachery was the foulest he had ever witnessed.

Milton Plastics was a reputed brand in consumer products, a family business that was run by Chiranjeev

Vaghani. Chiranjeev's elder brother called up Salem from the US and asked him to kidnap Chiranjeev. Salem harboured no great affection for the Milton Plastics director, nor did he owe him any allegiance, but in his village, Salem had been brought up with the idea that a younger brother is always the apple of one's eye.

And here was Vaghani calling him and offering him money to abduct his younger brother. The senior Vaghani had told Salem to demand Rs 25 crore as ransom for the safe return of Chiranjeev. This was gangster Babloo Srivastava's territory, and besides, high-profile abductions had never been Salem's thing. But the elder Vaghani brother seemed to trust Salem and his clout in Mumbai enough to offer him the job. The money on offer was tempting. So too was the fact that he was being asked to take the assignment even though he had decamped from Dubai. There's nothing quite like being in demand.

On 17 February 2000, four of Salem's men turned up at Chiranjeev's plush Malabar Hill home and picked him up. It was a simple enough task. Chiranjeev remained in the custody of his men for three days and his family was notified that the cost of his safe return was Rs 25 crore. Meanwhile, the Mumbai Police, routinely labelled (often by themselves) as the Scotland Yard of the east, remained clueless. Neither they nor the CBI had any clue about the whereabouts of the plastics baron. And even though Chiranjeev had five other brothers who were all very well off and had a fair bit of clout, no one could work out who had kidnapped him.

Eventually, after three days, Chiranjeev was allowed to return home safely after the ransom was paid. The Maharashtra deputy chief minister at the time, Chhagan Bhujbal, held a press conference and brazenly told the media that one of the six Vaghani brothers had been responsible for Chiranjeev's abduction. Some believed that the matter between the Vaghanis was settled with a sum of Rs 2 crore—a far cry from the Rs 25 crore that had been initially demanded.

Subsequently, the police and other investigating agencies made frantic efforts to hunt down the location from where the kidnapper's call originated. Some believed it may have come from Dubai, others thought London was the source. Finally, after checking phone records and tracing the numbers, the police concluded that the call had been made from a phone in Hong Kong. All along, Salem had been sitting comfortably in South Africa, monitoring the operation and ensuring that it was carried out smoothly.

Subsequent investigations revealed Salem's shrewd game plan in the sordid saga. Since his days of using police commando Rajesh Igwe as a sharpshooter, Salem knew that any new criminal enterprise needed the blessings of the police. To help with the Vaghani kidnapping, Salem had roped in a controversial police officer named Sanjay Shinde. Throughout the operation, Shinde remained in touch with Salem and kept relaying his instructions to the abductors.

Unknown to Shinde, Salem's phone was being tapped by the Crime Branch and police officers. Following this disclosure, the police department mooted the proposal for Shinde's dismissal, but let him off after a warning. Salem, meanwhile, had tasted success in a new territory and had finessed the art of using police officers to carry out his dirty work. He had now moved from using a constable to making a higher-level officer his accomplice. And for a pittance.

Yet, despite how effortless the whole abduction had been, the gangster was still uneasy. The job had taught him that there were no true friends or relatives in the cold world of business and that the only thing that truly mattered was money. Truly, *sabse bada rupaiya*.

He'd seen this phenomenon occurring in the past as well. When he had ordered a hit on builder Om Prakash Kukreja in late 1997, Salem had sent two of his most trusted hitmen, Salim Haddi and Rajesh Igwe, to kill him at his own residence. Moments after the duo entered Kukreja's apartment with loaded weapons, Om Prakash's younger brother had fled into his own bedroom and locked the door from inside. As Salem saw it, the younger brother had chosen to protect himself rather than save his kin, call the police or take on the attackers. Om Prakash Kukreja was killed in broad daylight and no one did a thing to save his life. This, as Salem perceived it, was what the world had turned into. Cowardice reigned supreme.

TWENTY

SAMEERA'S *SOUTEN*

NO WOMAN CAN TOLERATE ANOTHER WOMAN on her marital turf. So, it's no wonder that Sameera considered the other woman in her husband's life, the s*outen,* as the curse in her life. She felt that she had made a lot of sacrifices to keep the marriage steady. She had always known that Salem had a proclivity for bedding beautiful women, particularly starlets from the film industry, but she had allowed him to live his life as he saw fit. In fact, she knew about Monica and Salem, their growing intimacy and his huge efforts to promote her career. But she stayed calm and stoically accepted the truth. But now, Monica had entered Sameera's turf.

Salem had flown in to their palatial house at Jasmine Court, Fayetteville, in Georgia, unannounced and with

Monica, and had mooted the idea of the three of them living together. Sameera had by now become accustomed to her new life as Sabina Azmi. Salem had invested heavily in a supermarket-type grocery store so that Sameera could make a living. He had also transferred $170,000 (which in rupees was worth almost a crore) to ensure that she could maintain herself and their son. In America, she felt she could make a comfortable, safe life. But the second she saw Monica with her husband, she lost her temper. It was one thing to accept her husband's infidelities from a distance, another to confront it daily in her own home.

The problem was that most of Salem's money was in Sameera's name. Before leaving Dubai, the gangster had been careful to transfer funds from his bank in Sharjah to Sameera's accounts in Georgia. Salem had also invested in some properties in the USA in Sameera's name. He knew that business wasn't exactly booming, but these properties were set to appreciate in value. Both husband and wife expected to turn over a huge profit in time.

He thus needed Sameera to remain his wife formally and legally. The terms of the truce were that Salem and Monica would live far away from Sameera, but the latter would remain the gangster's wife. To seal the deal, Salem retook his marital vows, in Las Vegas, Nevada, on 4 March 2000 with Sameera. He then disposed of his huge Jasmine Court mansion and bought a modest house, Gadsen Walk Villa, in Duluth, Georgia, for Sameera and his son. Salem then moved out of the city and busied himself trying to settle down in Chicago.

Salem obtained a non-immigrant work visa as maintenance manager in a marine engineering company. He then used various other identities to set up businesses. In Dubai, Salem had met Farhat Husain, an event organizer, who had also become his financial and business adviser. Farhat advised him to buy a two-screen film theatre in Chicago which would only screen Indian and Pakistani movies. Since Chicago had a lot of Asians, the movie theatre business promised to be very profitable. Salem promptly launched a company by the name of Ariyan International that would deal with the overseas rights of Bollywood movies and organize events across the US. Under the aegis of the company, Salem bought a two-screen theatre by the name Da Plane.

In the meantime, after sorting out his personal life, Salem began to refocus his attention on the business side. Much to his relief, he realized around that time that despite his relocation and the unceremonious manner in which he had got up and left Dubai, his clout hadn't been affected even one tiny bit. He regularly met members of the Hindi film fraternity whenever they were in the States to shoot their films or perform at shows. He also began to get them together and organized shows of his own. Ariyan International handled the business side. Farhat Husain was of immense help to Salem. It was only a matter of time until the cash registers began ringing again. Once again, he began using the Captain sobriquet.

A number of big names from the industry used to come to pay obeisance to him regularly and were more than happy to shell out money and share their profits with him. For the next year and a half, life was extremely satisfying and pleasantly uneventful. An ongoing trend in Salem's life was that nothing ever seemed to last very long. And after dropping anchor in the US, it was perhaps a bit naive of him to imagine that such domestic bliss would last forever. But for a brief moment in his life, he believed he had truly settled down. It had taken some time and there were some rough edges that needed to be sanded down, but he was actually comfortable for the first time in a long time.

During this period, he moved a great deal of his money out of Dubai to the USA. The CBI, in their investigations (pieced together with the FBI), came across minute details of Salem's deals and money transactions in the US prior to 9/11. According to a top-secret CBI dossier, on 1 October 2001, a real estate appraiser, Buckhead Advisory Group Limited, valued Salem's immovable property at $1,325,000 (approximately Rs 6.5 crore). The valuation done by J. Michael Smith of Georgia raised the eyebrows of the FBI.

Salem owned five apartments in the US, besides a cinema and a few petrol pumps. He ran an automobile company and tyre company in the Middle East. These properties were largely acquired in the name of Ariyan International Private Limited, Salem's firm.

In January 2000, as Arsalan Mohsin Ali, resident of Commercial Area, Tariq Road, Karachi, he remitted $115,000 from his Standard Chartered Bank account in Sharjah to Wachovia Bank in the United States. Within three months, in April 2000, $200,000 from the Wachovia Bank account was sent to an account in Lasalle Bank, Schaumburg, Illinois. In June 2000, he transferred another $15,000 to a Citibank account in Chicago.

The CBI sleuths suspected that Salem also used Monica's account to move the money. In July 2000, Monica Bedi, resident of Eastwood Court, Schaumburg, Illinois, had $575,282 (Rs 2.6 crore) in her Citicorp account in San Antonio, Texas. Salem's bank account in Dubai showed that in October 2000, he had a balance of Rs 176.675 crore.

Apart from Salem's, the CBI recorded Monica's transactions as well. These were far smaller remittances as compared to Salem's, but were nevertheless interesting. In September 2001, Monica operated her Canara Bank account in Andheri to remit several transactions worth Rs 49,000 each which could only be collected by her parents in Norway. A family contact, Brij Arora, was used for the transaction through Credit Kassen Bank, Norway. In that period, she also operated a joint account owned by Ramesh Kumar and Monica Bedi. The account at HDFC Bank in Juhu–Versova Link Road in Mumbai had Rs 15 lakh as balance. The identity of the joint account holder with Monica Bedi—Ramesh Kumar—remains a mystery for the CBI sleuths.

A senior officer feels that it was Salem himself who masqueraded as Ramesh Kumar as he wanted to keep his finances under his own control and did not want Monica to have complete access to his monies. This has some credence because the CBI in its files has also noted that an application was submitted in the German consulate for a Germany visa for one B. Ramesh Kumar and his wife Monica Bedi. This was, incidentally, Salem's first-ever attempt to have a Hindu identity.

Far away from the likes of Shakeel, Anis, Dawood and all their goons, and with his finances consolidated, Salem began to believe he was finally on his way to building a peaceful and stable life with Monica. However, one man was watching them quietly. They might have escaped the scorching glare of rivals and detractors, but Salem and Monica could not skip the scrutiny of Neeraj Kumar, who was the joint director of the CBI in New Delhi. He received an intelligence input that Salem was trying to establish a base for himself in the US.

Neeraj Kumar got in touch with his counterpart at the FBI, but much to his chagrin, the FBI officer did not seem too keen on pursuing the lead. The reply that Kumar received from the FBI officer was something which he would never forget.

'Is this guy Al-Qaeda?' he was asked.

The US was yet to declare its war on terror against Al-Qaeda, but recent incidents such as the attacks on the American embassies in Dar-e-Salaam, Tanzania and Nairobi in August 1998 and more recently the fidayeen attack on the *USS Cole* on 12 October 2000 had already put the terror organization on their hit list. The US investigating agencies were programmed to hunt only for Al-Qaeda operatives across the globe.

On 11 September 2001, the world changed. Salem woke up reasonably early on that fateful Tuesday morning and switched on the television set with a yawn and a stretch. Flicking past channels, he noticed the same image being broadcast on each channel. Two iconic monoliths, one grey-white smear moving towards them. An explosion. Shock. He switched channels to see if he was imagining things, but it was the same clip looping on all news channels.

Walking through the fear-gripped streets of Chicago in the days to come, Salem could sense a more than palpable feeling of being watched or, more precisely, stared at. The anti-Muslim sentiment had turned into full-blown paranoia. Immigrants, especially recent immigrants, were being targeted. Muslim-owned shops were being vandalized, the term 'raghead' had turned into a racial slur as big as 'nigger' and even turbaned Sikhs were getting beaten up in the streets.

Salem was more nervous about being assaulted than worried about the plight of all Asian or Asian-looking people. He also knew that if he were to be admitted to a US hospital, they might run a background check on him and then discover that he wasn't Arsalan Ali, but Abu Salem—one of the accused in the 1993 Mumbai blasts.

The frequent visits and quizzing by the FBI, CIA and members of other investigating agencies were also putting him on edge. Money could not be a shield any more. With all the racial profiling, random violence and psychotic paranoia that was in the air, there was absolutely no way he was willing to risk his safety and that of Monica's in that country.

Within weeks, Salem had made up his mind.

'Start packing.'

The moment those words left Salem's mouth, Monica knew exactly why he was saying what he was saying. Despite feeling very comfortable in the United States with access to a life of luxury, she knew that they simply couldn't risk hanging around those parts any longer. Within weeks of 9/11, Salem and his lady love hopped on to the first flight out of O'Hare International Airport in Chicago and headed east.

Salem had always been highly adaptable. He had survived by being a product of change. Azamgarh to Mumbai to Dubai to the USA. So, this latest change wasn't really unsettling for him. It was Monica he was concerned about and of course, the threat from his ex-colleagues, friends and employers. But there was no time to mull over all that, he reckoned, as he began to take another look at a map of the world.

In the wake of the September 11 attacks, it wasn't just the United States, but Europe too that was on high alert. Also, anticipating that the CBI would have spread its men across the continent to take him out, Salem first landed in Oslo and spent six weeks with his parents-in-law. He then began chalking out his plan to look for another base.

TWENTY-ONE

SALEM UNDER SURVEILLANCE

IN ALL HIS FLIGHTS OF FANCY, Salem had never imagined that a day would come when he would rule as Bollywood's undisputed shah. The pervasiveness of his reign of terror was such that there was not a single industry professional who had not been threatened and intimidated by him or forced to part with money or business equity.

The gangster had threatened and extorted from virtually everyone—top film directors, producers, actors, distributors. In fact, even a lowly cameraman on a meagre salary or a director of photography would not be spared and would have to shell out Rs 5 lakh or so to buy peace.

When the Delhi Police put several phones under

electronic surveillance, some sensational disclosures came about. It was in November 1998 after listening in to the telephone calls of alleged Dawood frontman Romesh Sharma, the Delhi Police discovered his connections with Abu Salem.

The police had begun recording Sharma's phone calls from August 1998 and initially found him chatting with his girlfriend and people he boasted to about his political contacts.

The most vital breakthrough for the police came when they began tapping one particular phone that was used secretively and the number apparently known to only a very few people. Sharma used this number to call his friends in the underworld in Dubai. The police managed to record over fifty conversations between Sharma and Anis Ibrahim or Salem.

Over three months of tapping, the police heard Sharma and Salem discussing collection of cash for the imminent elections, plans to kill gangster Babloo Srivastava in jail, and Salem's attempts to extort money from actress Manisha Koirala.

The tapping continued until the police gathered enough evidence against Sharma, and finally arrested him on 20 October 1998. The transcripts of the conversations between Salem and Sharma indicated that the latter's fledgling party, the All India Bharatiya Congress Party, was poised to take off during the

Assembly polls. However, Sharma was facing an acute cash crunch and needed Salem to fund his campaign.

The following conversation took place on 18 October, barely two days before Sharma's arrest:

Sharma: *'Tangi hai. Maine seventy candidate laganein hain. Sixty crore chahiyein.'* (There is a paucity of funds. I have to field seventy candidates in the elections and I need Rs 60 crore).

Salem: *'Nahin, nahin, par tum baat kar lena.'* (No, no, but you talk about this [to the boss].)

Perhaps, Salem wanted Sharma to discuss the issue with Anis. For the Delhi Police, the most solid piece of intelligence that could potentially nail Sharma's links with the Salem gang was revealed in conversations on 1 October. Salem was calling Sharma to tell him about his attempt to extort money from Manisha Koirala. Incidentally, the Mumbai Police had already received complaints from her about the threatening calls she had received, and they were investigating. But they got their first clue from their counterparts in Delhi.

Salem: *'Maine phone kiya tha Manisha Koirala ko. Woh milee nahin. Maine kal chaar–paanch ladke bheje. Uske driver aur chowkidar ko peet diya.'* (I phoned Manisha Koirala, but she was not there. I sent four–five boys to her house. They beat up her driver and guard.)

Salem used to also share with Sharma details of major killings he was planning to carry out in and around Delhi. For instance, Salem revealed to Sharma that they were planning to kill Srivastava in Naini Jail, Allahabad. Salem told Sharma that it was a reprisal killing, revenge for the murder of Mirza Dilshad Beg in Nepal. Mirza was killed by Chhota Rajan and Srivastava in Kathmandu on 29 June 1998. However, Sharma assured Salem that he needn't worry nor send his men to kill Srivastava. His death would be orchestrated as part of a fake encounter by the Uttar Pradesh Police.

Salem said: '*Ek doosra kaam hone wala hai. Uska naam bataoonga.*' (Another job is going to be done. I will tell you the name.)'

Sharma: '*Kiska?*' (Whose?)

Salem: '*Mirza ka Babloo se milke kaam karaya tha. Uska badla lena hai.*' (Mirza was killed with the help of Babloo. We have to take revenge.)

Sharma: '*Uska kaam main karaa doonga UP Police se.* (I will get him killed by the UP Police.)

At least half a dozen tapes of such conversations were sealed and presented in court as part of evidence. There are also several tapes with recordings of harmless and innocuous conversations as well as a sheaf of handwritten transcripts, prepared either when the Crime Branch sleuths failed to switch on the recorder or when they ran out of tape.

Salem, who extorted money from the film fraternity, would also take his cue from the movies. The Mumbai

Crime Branch recorded a conversation in which Salem was directing five of his men and issuing instructions on how to attack Manmohan Shetty, the owner of the Adlabs chain of multiplexes.

Shetty was being threatened by Salem to hand over a large sum of money. Shetty had refused to buckle under the pressure, infuriating Salem who decided that the Adlabs man's intransigence would have to be punished. While talking to his men, he instructed them to watch the Sanjay Dutt starrer *Vaastav* and follow the modus operandi of a murder in the film.

Since these Azamgarh boys had no experience of killing anyone before, Salem had to describe each and every aspect of the hit job. As he discovered, the boys had not even done basic research on the target, and Salem began by describing Shetty's appearance to them, followed by the plan on how the killing was to be executed.

Salem: *'Imtiyaz, tum logon ne picture nahin dekhi kya,* Vaastav? Vaastav *nahin dekha kya Sanjay Dutt ki?'* (Imtiyaz, have you not seen the movie *Vaastav*? The Sanjay Dutt starrer *Vaastav*?)

Imtiyaz: *'Haan, bhai, dekhi hai.'* (Yes, bhai, we have seen it.)

Salem: *'Haan, toh vaisa hi karne ka hai, jaise picture mein kiya.'* (Yes, then do it the way it was done in the movie.)

Imtiyaz: '*Haan, aap befikar rahein, aap ko ek bhi shikayat ka mauka nahin milega. Hum log ko kuch bhi ho jaye, magar aap ko shikayat ka mauka nahin denge.*' (You don't worry, you will not have any complaints. Whatever may happen to us, we will not disappoint you.)

In the style of a particularly aggressive sports coach, Salem also used expletive-laden tirades to motivate his men the night before the planned attack on Manmohan Shetty. Salem exhorted his men not to leave the scene of the attack until they had completely exhausted their ammunition. The recorded conversation of this pep talk gave the Mumbai Police an insight into Salem's motivational speeches.

Salem: '*Aisa nahin ki ek–do firing kiya aur bhaag gaye. Maar dene ka. Poora khali karne ka. Phir nikalne ka. Choron ki tarah aisa kaam nahin karne ka ki do goli fire kiya aur bhaag gaye. Baat saaf hai, iske baad tum hero banoge.*' (Don't do a half-hearted job and fire a couple of rounds and escape. Shoot to kill. Finish all your bullets. Don't behave like cowards who fire two bullets and run away. It is clear you will become heroes after this.)

The conversation also revealed Salem's lack of ethics and his violation of the mafia code of never targeting a cop. Usually, no gunman was instructed to shoot a policeman howsoever extreme the circumstances. But Salem breached that basic code too.

Salem: '*Koi bhi police aa gaya, koi bhi saamne aa gaya, koi poochha ki kai ke liye khada hai, kyon khada hai, policewalla, to nikalo saaman aur dhan dhan usko maro . . . Poochha toh maar do usko. Yeh nahin ki aise hi khade hain. Agar poochha ki kaahe ke liye ghoom raha hai, kya kar raha hai, toh nikalne ka peechhe se. Aur khopdi mein san se dene ka.*' (If any cop comes or anyone asks you what you are doing there, take your gun and shoot him . . . Shoot anyone who questions your presence. Don't keep standing like a fool. The moment anyone questions you, get your gun and blast his head off.)

These conversations were recorded on 1 May 2001. Shetty was attacked the next day, 2 May. However, despite all these instructions and the motivational speeches, Salem's men botched up the assignment and Shetty was lucky to escape with injuries while the gunmen were arrested by the police.

TWENTY-TWO

CAUGHT OUT IN LISBON

SHAHZAD HAIDER, A SMALL-TIME ENTREPRENEUR, HAD made a new friend in Lisbon: Arsalan, a fellow Pakistani, distributed and exported Omax watches and he was very rich. The two got along like a house on fire and Shahzad considered Arsalan's beautiful Indian wife Sana as his sister. Shahzad had spent all his life in Geneva, Switzerland, but after marrying a Portuguese girl, he had settled down in Lisbon. The marriage gave him Portuguese citizenship and a passport. It was Shahzad, seeing Arsalan making trips throughout Europe looking for a place to settle down, who finally suggested that he make Lisbon his home. Shahzad also helped him through the process of acquiring Portuguese citizenship.

The two would usually meet at Arsalan's plush

apartment at Avenida Paulo VI in Zona L of the Chelas area in the wealthy suburbs of Lisbon. Shahzad was in awe of his new friend's lifestyle: his plush house, the expensive Jeep Mercedes WI which he knew would easily cost about 2 crore rupees in Pakistan, Arsalan's two diamond-studded rings which probably cost a few thousand dollars each . . .

But there was something about Arsalan's wealth that rubbed the Pakistani the wrong way. For instance, Shahzad would try to take Arsalan to small roadside delis for meals, but Arsalan always insisted on going to fancy restaurants. Shahzad disapproved of this, often punching Arsalan affectionately for squandering so much money. But Arsalan was determined to look and behave wealthy. No matter how much he tried to persuade his rich friend, Shahzad knew that Arsalan would never change—flaunting wealth would always be part and parcel of his friend's personality.

A massive shock lay in store for him. One day, Arsalan, with Shahzad next to him in the passenger seat, had just left Chelas and was driving on the roundabout at Rotunda de Cabo Ruivo. Suddenly, he hit the brakes so hard that a series of cars came to a screeching halt behind them. Before Shahzad could process what had happened, he saw armed police personnel and commandos surround them; a police jeep had also blocked them off from behind.

Shahzad didn't think they were the Policia de Seguranca Publica—the civilian police that worked in urban areas; their uniform was a light blue shirt, dark blue tie and trousers and a blue cap. Arsalan's car, on the other hand, was surrounded by men in black commando uniforms and balaclavas that left only their eyes visible. They were from the Policia Judiciara, which only dealt with major criminal cases. Why were they after Arsalan?

Inspector Pereira Cristovao flashed his badge and ID, and loudly repeated, 'Police, Police, Police.' Arsalan and Shahzad were instructed to step out of the car slowly with their hands in the air. Once they were out, the commandos forced them to bend face down on the bonnet of their car and they were then handcuffed behind their backs. Shahzad tried to engage their chief in conversation and convince him that there was some mix-up. The chief warmed up to Shahzad when he heard him speak in Portuguese. But he told Shahzad that his friend was actually a man who had a red-corner alert notice from Interpol. This man was no Pakistani called Arsalan. He was Abu Salem and he was a terrorist wanted by the Indian police for his involvement in the Mumbai blasts.

Salem used the unwitting distraction created by Shahzad's conversation with the chief to move closer to the roundabout and surreptitiously remove both his diamond rings and drop them in the shrubbery. He knew those rings were valued at over $25,000, worth lakhs in Indian currency, and did not want the police to seize them. Salem later told Monica's brother Bobby to retrieve the rings.

The two men were taken to the police headquarters, known as the Policia Judiciara National, which works under the aegis of the Ministry of Justice. Salem was also charged for crashing his vehicle into a police van despite repeated warnings and for resisting arrest. Both these charges were highly unlikely ones—Salem had always behaved discreetly outside India and he wouldn't have dreamed of defying a cop or even banging against his vehicle.

Subsequently, a group of officers left for Salem's residence in Avenida Paulo VI at Chelas and arrested Monica Bedi, living under the identity of Sana Kamil Malik. They searched the house in Monica's presence and found a driver by the name of Shaikh Afzal sleeping in one of the rooms. They also seized several Indian passports and various visas—Swiss, American, Canadian, British, Schengen and Portuguese—as well as several Lufthansa tickets which indicated trips between Oslo and Lisbon, and Oslo and Frankfurt, train tickets between Stuttgart and Frankfurt, handwritten details of cash transactions, and bank statements. The team, led by Inspector Pereira Cristovao and agents Rui Mendao, Nuno Santos and Nuno Henriques, also found cash which included forty-nine bills of $100 denomination, and 2035 Indian rupees. They also found marriage documents of Arsalan Mohsin Ali with Deolinda Maria, and of Shahzad Haider with Sana Kamil Malik.

Since his departure from Chicago in October the previous year, Salem had been scouring Europe for a place to call home, even as he switched identities while in each country. The past year may have been unstable, but it was also a very happy and romantic time in his relationship with Monica. They were far from the law enforcement agencies, his rivals and enemies. And best of all, they were a whole ocean away from Sameera and her judgemental glare. The couple got married on 20 November 2001. They spent six weeks with Monica's family in Norway and then left on a longish honeymoon. For Salem, this was his third marriage, although he claims that Monica was his second wife.

The couple settled initially in Norway. Monica's familiarity with the place obviously helped, as did the fact that they were completely unknown to the locals. That was the first time that Salem realized that Monica was taking his money without permission. This led to fights between them—with Salem revealing his true colours and becoming violent with Monica as he had been with Sameera. But he always took the initiative of making up with his beautiful new wife, whereas he would ignore Sameera for days. Salem would also lavish expensive gifts on her and take her to new places, two things that women generally like. The constant travelling also helped them stay below the radar. Monica and Salem would drive up and down the continent, looking for a place to call home, because Norway was always only a makeshift residence. They drove to Switzerland, Spain and Germany, but nothing seemed right.

Salem kept up his Bollywood connections in the meantime, meeting all the stars who would come to shoot in Switzerland. As usual, he took the identity of Arsalan while socializing with the film world. It was in this context that he met Shahzad who still had a base and substantial contacts in Geneva. Shahzad persuaded him to settle down in Lisbon and they moved to the Portuguese capital, renting a massive apartment stocked with a 24/7 team of servants, drivers, butlers, etc. And after all these years, Salem finally had a garage packed with amazing cars. This was to be a short-lived phase of peace and comfort. For Salem, happiness was always a temporary state.

In the meantime, Shahzad was helping them with the paperwork. He told Salem that he and Monica would have to briefly marry citizens of Portugal which would earn them that much-desired residence card. After that, they could even apply for citizenship. And so, Shahzad had a civil marriage with Monica, while Salem married Deolinda Maria. Deolinda was paid 3000 euros, while Shahzad was paid 4500 euros for their services.

Shahzad was horrified when he discovered that the man who had been his bosom pal for the last ten months and who had behaved so warmly, taking his ribbing and his punches sportingly, was actually a dreaded don from India. The man could put a chameleon to shame. Salem had perfected the art of being the globetrotting bluffmaster who could switch identities at the drop of a hat. For instance, to complete the cover of being Danish Beg, Salem also got a marksheet from Mumbai University which showed that he was a commerce graduate and had passed with flying colours. His master creation was Arsalan Ali and he had put in a lot of detail to this identity. Arsalan had both an address and parentage—he was apparently born to Mohsin Ali and Sultana Ali, both from Tariq Road, Karachi. Arsalan had also previously married Yasmeen on 30 August 1996. But then, due to their relationship breaking down, he had to divorce her on 15 February 2000. Arsalan had apparently given *talaq-baen* (a sort of irrevocable divorce which is normally issued in multiple sittings) to Yasmeen so that she could not claim any part of his inheritance.

He had then married Sana Malik (alias Monica) for a *mehr* (alimony) of Rs 50,000 in Karachi. The nikah was recited by Mohammad Jameel Hafiz Ghulami. The *qazi* who represented Sana Malik was Mohammad Azam Ata

Mohammad. The nikah was solemnized on 20 August 2001. The papers for the ceremony were notarized by advocate Ashraf Ali of City Court, Pakistan, and was ratified by Zahid Masud, the section officer at the Ministry of Foreign Affairs, Camp Office, Karachi. In the papers, Sana Malik was a resident of Commercial Area, Karachi. And since it is mandatory to mention on the *nikahnama* whether the bride was previously married or unmarried, the column mentions that she was a virgin. It was signed by her.

There is no evidence if the Karachi nikah ever happened—we don't know if the couple travelled to Pakistan during the period. However, Salem considers the details of this marriage to be sacrosanct, although Monica does not. Monica, according to a letter she wrote to Salem in jail, believed her wedding took place on 20 November 2001 in Oslo. In fact, all these details worked against Salem and Monica when he was prosecuted in Lisbon. One of the documents that the CBI dug up and presented in court was the one showing Salem's identity as Ramesh Kumar. Ramesh Kumar had made an application in the German consulate in Dubai, seeking a visa for his wife, Monica Bedi. So, Monica Bedi could not be Sana Malik, wife of Arsalan, nor could she then be Monica, wife of Ramesh Kumar, or Bhopal resident Fauzia Usman. All inconsistencies sealed Salem's fate in Lisbon.

On 18 September 2002, Salem was thrown into

prison, and the Indian authorities were duly notified. Once in prison, Salem obsessed about how they had known he was Abu Salem. Had they been tracking him for some time? And who had ratted on him? Was he caught because he had made a stupid error post the September 11 attacks? As he was making plans to flee the USA, he had asked one of his trusted associates in the country to transfer all his funds to his accounts in Europe. He had, however, failed to factor in Uncle Sam breathing down his neck. Huge money transfers across continents were bound to show up on investigating agencies' radars. Once, Salem's lackey in Dubai had told him, *'Anis bhai ne abhi aapka peechha nahin chhoda hai, bhai.'* (Anis has not stopped chasing you.) The phone call simultaneously made his blood turn to ice and set it aflame. Was it Anis who had given his location to the cops? But there was no way that Anis could have known where he was hiding.

Salem had never liked Monica talking to her friends on a cell phone. He suspected that the intelligence agencies were equipped to track people through mobile phones. Had Monica alerted the authorities because she was tired of living the life of a fugitive? Monica often told Salem that she wanted to go back to India and live like an ordinary person. Salem usually laughed it off. One last suspicion kept nagging Salem's mind. What if it was Sameera? She was hurt and angry with him.

She knew that once he was thrown behind bars, all his money would be hers. The more he thought of this, the more convinced he was that it was Sameera who had betrayed him. She had taken her revenge.

TWENTY-THREE

THE LISBON INCARCERATION

ESTABELECIMENTO PRISIONAL DE LISBOA, OR THE EPL, was like a fortress, an architectural marvel actually. The façade is imposing, as if it is intended to crush the spirit of the prisoners who stand in front of the gates, fearfully waiting to enter. But curiously, the main arch with its impressive wrought-iron gates actually opens into the jail's hospital, right next to the entrance. Famous Indian prisons such as Tihar in New Delhi or Mumbai's Central Prison pale in comparison to the EPL. The only Indian prison that can compare with its architecture and grandeur is perhaps the Cellular Jail, or Kālā Panī, in the Andaman islands. Kālā Panī is a British-era structure built in 1896 and probably that explains why it shares some similarities with the EPL, which was constructed in 1884.

For those who haven't seen prisons in real life, the EPL is something like the jails depicted in Hollywood movies such as *The Shawshank Redemption* or the more recent Sylvester Stallone–Arnold Schwarzenegger vehicle *The Escape Plan*. It was built for a total of 887 inmates, but is crammed with over 2000 prisoners at any point of time, just like the overcrowded Indian jails. When Salem walked into the prison, he was one of the very few Asians there.

He was kept in the high-security area known as 'the Pavilion' because he was facing terror charges. But once inside, he found this jail to be no different from jails he had heard about back home. These cells too were in terrible condition—plaster peeling everywhere, broken windows, inadequate lighting, and old, stinking mattresses. Salem cursed his luck at the sight of such a wretched existence. Life had taken a 180-degree turn for him in the space of a year.

News of his dramatic arrest in Lisbon grabbed headlines in all the local papers and dominated most of the front pages of Mumbai's newspapers too. The response in India varied from disbelief and scepticism to total celebration. The builder community and Bollywood fraternity heaved a sigh of relief. Some actually threw parties to celebrate. No other underworld character's downfall had resulted in so much happiness.

Prior to Salem's arrest in Lisbon, other mafia arrests

overseas included Iqbal Mirchi's detention in London in 1995 and Anis Ibrahim's detention in Bahrain the same year. Both were subsequently released due to technical complications in their documents. In fact, Salem had himself managed to wriggle out of detention in Dubai soon after the Gulshan Kumar killing in 1997. In 1995, Babloo Srivastava, the kingpin of abduction rackets in Delhi, was successfully extradited from Singapore, but it had been a long time since such a big fish had been caught.

Soon after the arrests, the additional director of the CBI, Vijay Shankar, made a trip to Lisbon to confirm and coordinate with the Portuguese authorities. Having burnt their fingers twice in the past, the CBI was not willing to let go of their wanted man this time. They swung into action and began putting together all the documents and paperwork needed for Salem's extradition to India. The government was also totally prepared this time. On 13 December 2002, within two months of Salem's arrest, Omar Abdullah, who was the junior minister in the Ministry of External Affairs, sent a requisition letter for Salem's and Monica's extradition from Portugal. Salem's case was transferred from the Policia Judiciara to the Departamento Central de Investigacao E Accao Penal (DCIAP), or Central Investigation and Penal Action Department, the local counterpart of the CBI in Portugal. This made coordination easier, given that both were apex bodies and nodal agencies for their respective countries.

Salem was now in the vortex of long and tedious extradition proceedings between Portugal and India. India does not have an extradition treaty with Portugal. Among the European countries, France, Germany and Bulgaria are the only ones that have signed such a treaty with India. Portugal, on the other hand, is in disagreement with India's system of death penalty, having banned state executions as far back as 1867. As a result, the Portuguese government was not keen on entertaining Indian requests for extradition. The DCIAP had also not found Salem guilty of anything that would constitute a major crime in Portugal or warrant his extradition—he was being tried for forgery and falsification of documents. But when the Indian government insisted that Salem was an accused in the serial blasts of 1993, the Portugal government softened its stand and agreed.

However, Portugal was not willing to send Salem back until the Indian government gave firm assurances, in writing, that the Indian courts would neither award the death penalty to Salem nor give him a jail sentence longer than twenty-five years. L.K. Advani, the then deputy prime minister who also held the home ministry portfolio, wrote a letter to Antonio Martins da Cruz, Portugal's minister for foreign affairs, promising that the Indian state would keep to these terms. The letter was personally signed by L.K. Advani, and not by any bureaucrat or junior minister. This eased the anxiety of the Portuguese government.

Initially, Salem was detained for three months, but his detention was continually extended. After the third extension, the Portuguese court declared its verdict, finding Salem and Monica guilty on several counts of forgery and for the use of forged documents. Salem was held guilty on three counts by the Sixth Penal Court of Lisbon and sentenced to three years in prison. He was given two years for resisting arrest and assaulting a police officer on duty. A third year was added for perjury, after his false depositions before a court about being a Pakistani national called Arsalan Mohsin Ali.

Salem had initially stuck to his line of being Arsalan until the Indian government exposed his real identity by producing his fingerprints taken after he was picked up by the D.N. Nagar cops. This amounted to perjury in Portuguese courts. It also undermined Salem's case and dented his standing with the DCIAP. Until then, the authorities had vociferously supported Salem against the Indian government, especially since he and Monica had obtained Portuguese residential permit through legal means. Under Portuguese law, these terms of imprisonment add up to six years, but the court reduced them to four and a half years. Monica too was convicted of forgery, but the court gave her a lesser sentence of two years as Salem confessed to having acquired the forged documents for her.

Salem tried to make the best of prison life. His cellmate was an Italian drug peddler named Roberto Giovanni who was accused of cocaine trafficking. Salem's lack of fluency in English turned out to be a major hurdle in communicating with Giovanni, but the two were communicating in sign language, broken English and Salem's smattering of Portuguese. They got along famously. Roberto showed photographs of his family to Salem, reviving the dormant paternal instinct in the don. Salem started to think about his son Amir, who was more than five years old now. He had not seen him in a very long time and asked his Chicago contacts to get him a photo of the boy. He pasted the photograph on the wall of his cell and would continuously look at it. The image became Salem's crutch during his periods of loneliness.

Like all high-security prisons, the EPL too forbade any written communication between prisoners. But Monica managed to write letters to Salem and have them smuggled to him. Salem sought solace in Monica's regular letters, reading them over and over again. If she failed to write to him or the letter was delayed, he would be extremely upset. The letters would go on to reveal an astonishing level of intimacy and love between the two.

TWENTY-FOUR

LOVE AND LONGING IN LISBON

SALEM HAD ENJOYED WHAT SOME MIGHT describe as a hyperactive sex life. He is believed to have taken a number of stars and starlets to bed, including a former beauty queen and countless silver-screen aspirants. But it was Monica who completely changed the parameters of physical intimacy for him. It was also Monica who taught him to love.

Alone in jail, it was Monica's steady flow of highly emotional and sexually explicit letters that kept him going. Monica made these cards by hand, carefully crafting them for occasions such as their anniversary, his birthday or Eid. Each day, prison guards would walk past the cells with a duffel bag full of mail for the inmates. Perhaps it was sixth sense or simply the connection he shared with Monica, but Salem invariably had this feeling of warmth in the pit of his stomach that told him there was a letter or a card for him on a given day.

Monica wrote to her lover in Hindi—we don't know if this was because Salem's understanding of English was rudimentary and she had to meet him halfway or whether she was capable of expressing herself better in the language or if Hindi was just a good way to keep her words from the prying eyes of the prison guards. In her letters, Monica spoke of her love for him and remembered the events of their past, both affectionate and amorous, in vivid detail.

The couple spent three wedding anniversaries in jail. During this time they couldn't see each other for more than half an hour a week. But as time passed, even these brief meetings began to grow less frequent. Monica's letters which in the early days dripped with love, affection, devotion, desire and lust, over time began to seem extremely colourless, prosaic and, worst of all, distant. In July 2005, Monica wrote her last letter to Salem. They were adrift.

Monica had hit rock bottom with her imprisonment. She had dreamt of becoming a top actress in Bollywood and here she was, reduced to being an accomplice of India's most wanted ganglord. From hobnobbing with Bollywood stars, she was now rubbing shoulders with hard-core criminals in jail. The young woman felt humiliated, ruined and devastated. The Christian missionaries who visited prisoners converted her to Christianity during this vulnerable moment. Monica found peace in the Bible and a stability she had lost. She stopped greeting Salem with the word 'Salaam'—something that he loved—and referring to Allah as her God. Salem was totally mystified at her transformation.

When Monica heard about the extradition proceedings, she yearned to return to India, while Salem was fighting the Indian government's moves tooth and nail. Salem would never understand how the woman who wouldn't be turned away from him by his temper, his violence or his ill treatment had gone so far away from him in a few years of separation and a jail term.

TWENTY-FIVE

THE JOURNEY BACK

ONE NOVEMBER AFTERNOON IN 2005, FOUR heavily guarded cars and jeeps with armed commandos on either side made their way towards a massive aircraft that was carrying a very special cargo: Abu Salem and his wife or girlfriend Monica Bedi.

Devendra Pardesi, the deputy superintendent of police of the Special Task Force of the CBI, had handled innumerable tough cases and far tougher criminals. But this case seemed a bit unreal. The man that the Portuguese police was handing over just didn't fit the bill of one of India's most dreaded gangsters who had masterminded some of the most gruesome murders in the annals of Mumbai crime.

The occupant of the second car soon stepped out

of her vehicle. Dressed in a T-shirt and a pair of jeans, Monica Bedi looked more suited to walk down a ramp at a fashion show. With the air of a starlet, she seemed to fit the bill of a gangster's moll. Unlike Salem, she was not smiling, and apprehension was written clearly across her face, and she clutched at a Bible for dearly life. To Pardesi, it looked like the usual story. A pretty girl with dreams of stardom, falling for the wrong man, spending time in the wrong company, fleeing the country and ending up being extradited home like a criminal.

Pardesi's boss, Deputy Inspector General Om Prakash Chhatwal, signed on the official documents. Before the ink had even dried, Pardesi approached the nervously smiling man and said, '*Kyon be? Tu hi Abu Salem hai?*'

Salem became a bit wary at this point and his nervousness gave way to raw, unbridled fear: '*Kya aap Crime Branch se hain?*'

The fear was palpable.

'*Nahin, hum CBI se hain,*' came the reply.

To any normal human being, being in CBI custody would be as bad as Crime Branch custody, but Salem became completely relaxed and replied, '*Phir chalo, saab. Apne watan chalna hai.*'

It was not a formal conversation, but since both parties knew the purpose of the meeting, there didn't seem to be any point in waiting. The motley group now walked towards the Indian Air Force's massive Russian-made cargo plane waiting for them.

The Indian government had finally managed to extradite Salem and Monica after a protracted legal battle that had lasted over three years and two months. It had registered over seventy-two cases of murder, abduction, attempt to murder and extortion against Salem. But a Portugal court consented to Salem's prosecution in only nine cases: three passport forgery cases in Lucknow, Hyderabad and Bhopal; three extortion cases in New Delhi; and three cases of the Mumbai Police, including the murder of builder Pradeep Jain, the murder of Manisha Koirala's secretary Ajit Diwani and the weapons delivery case of the serial blasts of 1993. Ironically, the Mumbai Police was restrained from prosecuting Salem in the Gulshan Kumar case or in the cases involving attacks on other film personalities such as Subhash Ghai, Rajiv Rai and Rakesh Roshan, or in the conspiracy to kill Aamir Khan, Manisha Koirala and Ashutosh Gowariker.

Salem was not happy about going back to India. He knew that his chances of getting out of a Portugal jail in a few years' time were much better than rotting in Indian jails for God knows how long. However, the Indian government had made this case a prestige issue and this time they were determined not to lose in an international court. They were willing to sign any deal or agree to any term. That's why they agreed to the Portuguese court even when it rejected sixty-three cases and took up only nine. They just wanted Salem back in India.

The mission to bring Salem back to Mumbai from Lisbon was a clandestine operation, planned to precision. The CBI agents, aware of the possibility of political pressure derailing their plans, had been extra careful. Resisting all sorts of bureaucratic pressures and maintaining secrecy at all levels, finally the CBI had managed to put Salem on a plane to Mumbai. It had to be an Air Force plane, because a civilian aircraft would have been a dead giveaway.

The aircraft was as different as it could be from a civilian aircraft. Never mind tray tables and in-flight meals, the aircraft's wide body held no interiors. It was like a giant room with metal benches on the sides. Ropes dangled from the ceiling and a mini crane stuck out like a sore thumb at the far end of the cargo hold. A makeshift urinal was all it had in terms of toilet facilities. This was a very different kind of air travel than what Salem was used to.

In the plane, Salem was handcuffed to the side of one of the metal benches, with a thick curtain separating him from his lady love. As he would later find out, those handcuffs were not intended to prevent Salem's escape; rather they were in place to stop him from harming himself. A suicide while being escorted back to India would have destroyed the CBI and its reputation.

The CBI wanted to handle this whole imbroglio just right and not leave any room for error. Were something to happen to Salem, they would never be able to recover from the scandal. Human rights activists would roast them alive.

'*Saab, mujhe ek baar Monica se milne do na,*' pleaded Salem.

'Don't you dare move from where you are,' said Pardesi gruffly.

The cargo plane was now in the air and Salem was too dejected to look at the country he was leaving behind. The next four hours felt like an eternity; meanwhile, the aircraft landed at Cairo International Airport to be refuelled. Chhatwal and Pardesi saw this as a perfect time to stretch their legs. This courtesy was not extended to Salem. After a two-hour halt, the plane was on its way to Mumbai.

After years on the run from the police, Anis, and perhaps even from himself, Salem yearned for a chat with someone. And so he began to speak freely with Pardesi and related to him tales of his family and Monica. She, on the other hand, had no desire to speak at all and buried herself in her Bible.

The tyres of the huge cargo plane hit the tarmac at Mumbai's Sahar International Airport at 7.30 a.m., much to the relief of Pardesi and Chhatwal. They had managed to bring Salem home without a hitch. At the airport, they were greeted by agents from the IB who swiftly took Salem to one side and grilled him for over an hour and a half.

Eventually, the CBI ran out of patience and told the IB officials to back off. Salem and Monica were escorted out of the airport in a Central Industrial Security Force (CISF) jeep. The CISF is a paramilitary force assigned the task of protecting airports across the country. Once outside the airport, they were put in a different vehicle and taken across town to a vacant bungalow—normally used by a minister—in Nariman Point. This was the makeshift office of the CBI Special Task Force investigating the Mumbai serial blasts of 1993.

Abu Salem had returned to Mumbai. He was finally back in the city that taught him his trade and made him the dreaded and feared gangster that he was.

TWENTY-SIX

THE NEW JERSEY CONNECTION

THE COURTROOM WAS PACKED TO THE rafters. The tension was palpable.

The hundred accused of the Mumbai serial blasts were present in the court and so were over a dozen lawyers and several CBI officers. The specially designated TADA courtroom wore an air of eerie grimness.

At the centre of attention were two distinctly different men, regarded as frenemies of sorts. Film actor Sanjay Dutt was riding high on the recent success of *Munnabhai MBBS*—his comeback vehicle to stardom. The other was Salem—clean-shaven, nattily dressed, wearing nice shoes, sporting gelled hair and smelling of expensive cologne, quite in contrast to the morose and weary Sanjay. Salem, unlike his former friend, was smiling, displaying his characteristic chirpy disposition.

Sanjay and Salem were of course good friends once upon a time—Salem in complete awe of Sanjay and the star enjoying the attention. The running joke in the Mumbai underworld had been that Salem did not bathe for three days after having delivered the AK-56 to Sanjay Dutt before the riots. After that, the two had kept in touch over the phone and met several times in Dubai during Sanjay's foreign shoots or events. Their friendship was in fact a much-discussed subject within the Bollywood–mafia circles.

But times change. Those who know Sanjay claimed he had grown uncomfortable with Salem. Salem often used intimidation and coercion to retain Sanjay as a friend, something the star detested. It wasn't the same case with Chhota Shakeel, Salem's arch-enemy and Dawood Ibrahim's right-hand man, with whom Sanjay shared an easy, comfortable equation. A telephone conversation recorded on 14 July 2002 exposed Sanjay Dutt's connections with Shakeel. The transcripts would later be produced in the MCOCA (Maharashtra Control of Organized Crime Act) court where Sanjay would have to explain them away by saying he was too drunk and didn't have the slightest clue who he was talking to.

Salem had by then fallen out with his former boss Anis Ibrahim and was aware that he and Shakeel were stalking him at every turn. What he did not know was that they had also allegedly involved his one-time friend Sanjay Dutt in a plot to eliminate him in New Jersey. For the record, the actor has always denied his involvement in such a conspiracy.

According to unconfirmed reports, Salem had told his old friend Sanjay that he would attend one of the star-studded live Bollywood shows in New Jersey. Salem wanted to drop by and say hello to Sanjay and his other 'friends' in Bollywood. After all, this was 2001 and he was living inconspicuously in the US. Not many in Bollywood knew that Salem was trying to settle down in Chicago and was making efforts to extend his base to Los Angeles and New Jersey.

Salem had confided only in Sanjay about his plans to attend the event. Maybe he wanted to make it seem like a casual visit to a 'Bollywood night' while he was on a trip to the US, and wanted to give away nothing about his whereabouts in the country. At the very last minute, however, the gangster received some chilling intelligence and cancelled his visit to the event. Chhota Shakeel had hatched a plot to kill Salem in New Jersey, he was told. Shakeel's gunmen had conducted a recce of the stadium and were planning to strike as soon as Salem appeared at the glittering event. Salem had heard that it was Sanjay who had tipped Shakeel off about his expected presence at the event.

Salem was only too well aware of Shakeel's skills and

resourcefulness, and how well he could plan an attack. Only a few months ago, on 15 September 2000, Shakeel had orchestrated an audacious attack on Chhota Rajan in his den in Bangkok. Rajan had survived by the skin of his teeth. Salem decided to cancel his visit to New Jersey, but harboured a massive grudge against Sanjay and had decided to punish him for his treachery and betrayal.

A few months later, Salem organized four gunmen to 'take care of' Sanjay. The actor was in Goa at the time, along with friend and director of *Kaante*, Sanjay Gupta, known to him as Gups. Salem's instructions to his boys were clear: Go after Sanjay and kill him in Goa or at Mumbai airport upon his return. But Sanjay and Gups heard of the planned hit and desperately began working the phones to get help. They asked several friends of Salem's to mediate, but these men found Salem in no mood to forgive Sanjay Dutt.

Sanjay and Gups remained holed up in the hotel room until they managed to get hold of a close friend of Salem's in Mumbai by the name of Akbar Khan. This man had helped Salem in the days when the don was on the run from the Mumbai Police after the serial blasts. Khan had helped Salem cross the border and had even driven him to Kathmandu in his own car. It was a huge risk for him to take and Salem was so grateful to Khan that he never refused him a thing.

When Gups asked Khan to intervene, the latter agreed. After all, who would not want to oblige a successful and affluent film-maker? Khan called up Salem and asked him to rein in his shooters. Salem was furious, but also couldn't say no to Khan. He told him that his hitmen would not touch the two Sanjays so long as they travelled in Khan's car. The news of amnesty was conveyed to the beleaguered actor–director duo, much to their immense relief. They managed to reach Mumbai airport and Khan ferried them across town in his Hyundai Santro, saving them from the wrath of Salem and his shooters.

Khan was no Good Samaritan. Over the next few months, he regularly visited Sanjay Gupta's plush office in Lokhandwala and took lakhs of rupees for something or the other, part of the unwritten price for his help. Gupta resented it, but shelled out the money quietly. He could hardly irk Khan and invite bad luck home. While Khan extracted hard cash from Gupta, he ensured that Sanjay Dutt, whose market price at the time was a couple of crores per film, worked in his own movie for free. Market analysts dubbed the movie as the most disastrous of Sanjay's career and wondered what made him take up the movie just as his career was peaking.

Salem later boasted that he decided to forgive Sanjay because the actor had called him on his satellite phone (which used to cost Rs 1000 per minute for a call) and tearfully sought his forgiveness. Salem would boast about this incident, saying to his audience that he had decided to forget Sanjay's betrayal out of the goodness of his heart.

Two things were clear from these incidents: firstly, Salem and Sanjay were no longer friends. Two, Salem was gunning for Sanjay. The veracity of Salem's claim of forgiving Sanjay could never be verified though. That's why in court, the actor decided to avoid Salem and preferred to take a seat on the last bench along with a few of the accused. The officers from the ATS who had surrounded Salem from all sides (for his own safety) were also there to ensure that Salem did not abuse Sanjay in any way.

Soon after the serial blasts case charge sheet was filed on 4 November 1993 at the TADA court (in the Mumbai sessions court near Colaba), the city police were faced with the massive problem of security. The case involved over two hundred accused, over a thousand witnesses, and scores of lawyers and police personnel.

It was going to be a major challenge to ferry all these accused from Arthur Road Jail to Colaba on a daily basis. This would involve several dozen vehicles and complicated security paraphernalia. Any security glitch would easily result in a major catastrophe for the city which was still recovering from the serial blasts. The police were not willing to take any chances.

So, in an unprecedented step, the state government vacated a major portion of the Arthur Road Jail and dedicated it for the specially designated TADA court meant only for the serial blasts trial. This arrangement allowed the accused to meet their lawyers in the court premises itself. Relatives could also drop in to meet the accused. This section of the jail sprawled across acres of land and some of the accused even discovered nooks and crannies to grab an intimate moment or two with their wives, right within the court premises.

But Sanjay, of course, was too prominent a personality to hide in some secluded corner. He knew that he had to go through the motions of paying obeisance to the don. During the recess, several accused hugged Salem and greeted him with extreme cordiality, some of them fawning over him. Sanjay remained standing in a corner. Salem was, in fact, eager to meet Sanjay or at least give him his famous glare that was capable of having a spine-chilling effect on the recipient. Eventually, as he came down the stairs along with his ATS escorts, he spotted Sanjay standing there. It was quite an awkward moment for Sanjay, although Salem kept smiling.

Not knowing what to say to dispel the awkwardness, Sanjay took the initiative and said, *'Salaam alaikum, bhai.'* Salem promptly replied, *'Walaikum salaam.'* Sanjay then asked, *'Khairiyat?'* Salem merely nodded to this question about his well-being and moved on.

The actor heaved a sigh of relief—the storm had passed and all was well.

Having arrived in Mumbai on 10 November 2005, Salem was produced in the TADA court the next day. He preferred not to inform his family members of his arrival. At the time, he did not have a lawyer, but several lawyers of varying levels of skill were jostling for his attention. Salem was remanded to custody and Judge Pramod Kode was more than fair to him. Salem was allowed home food and other facilities during his time in the jail. Special Public Prosecutor Ujjwal Nikam told the court that the CBI's Special Task Force which was spearheading the prosecution would file a supplementary charge sheet against Salem in the next thirty days. Judge Kode gave his nod for the time period.

Salem was kept in the high-security *anda* cell—the egg-shaped enclosure in Arthur Road Jail—to protect him from any hostile gang rivals among the inmates. He hated it. Cramped space, discourteous staff, stinking toilets, mosquitoes, no bedsheets, and other such miseries threatened to make his incarceration insufferable. Slowly though, Salem began to settle in, especially when he came to the realization that jail authorities react positively to the stature and wealth of gang members. With everyone being respectful to Salem, he started enjoying his time in jail. The only thing Salem was missing was Monica and her love.

TWENTY-SEVEN

SAMEERA LASHES OUT

SAMEERA JUMANI FILED FOR EX PARTE divorce from Salem exactly a month after his arrest in Lisbon, on 20 October 2005. The divorce suit was filed in the superior court of Gwinnett County, Georgia, USA. It was technically called the Marital Settlement Agreement where Sameera was the plaintiff; she filed it as Sabina Arsalan Ali against her defendant husband Abu Salem, who was identified as Arsalan Mohsin Ali, a Pakistani. The court dissolved the marriage and Sabina Ali was restored to her maiden name Sabina Azmi. It was the same fictitious identity that she had assumed when she had escaped from Mumbai in 1993.

Salem executed a general power of attorney through an affidavit, as he was in prison. The power of attorney was meant to allow her to organize transfers of Salem's property to herself. Salem clarified that he had done this freely and voluntarily for the support and benefit of his eight-year-old son, Amir. The decree clearly mentioned that Salem and Sameera were married on 5 January 1991 in Mumbai and retook their marriage vows on 4 March 2000 in Las Vegas, Nevada. It said, 'The parties lived together as husband and wife until on or about March 05, 2001, when the defendant, without plaintiff, moved to Lisbon, Portugal, and the parties have remained in a bona fide state of separation ever since.' The marriage had lasted exactly ten years and two months.

Sheela Raval, one-time Editor Investigations with *Star News*, was in the US doing a story on Salem when the Portugal government was packing him off and Monica. She decided to track down Salem's first wife and after several wild goose chases, landed at Sameera's Georgia residence. Sheela said, 'Sameera was terrified of her abusive husband's wrath and yet she was eager to tell her story as she wanted the truth to come out. She firmly believed that the real perpetrator was let off the hook.'

Sheela spoke to Sameera exclusively for six hours on various issues. The interview was aired on 18 November 2005 under the headlines *Mera Pati Abu Salem* and *Salem's Biwi No. 1*. This is the only instance when Sameera bared her heart to a journalist and candidly spoke about Salem, giving an insight into his mind and personality.

During the extensive interview, Sameera spoke about her 'forced' marriage to Salem, her relations with him, Monica Bedi's role in their married life and the looming shadow of Dawood Ibrahim on Salem's life. She described Salem's insecurities and drew a picture of the gangster as a coward. She distanced herself from his activities, indicating that Monica was his accomplice while she was not connected with his work. She also said that she had been routinely beaten up by Salem and that he was a violent, 'psychotic man'. She confirmed that Salem used to beat up Monica as well. 'What Monica experienced for two years, I experienced for fifteen,' she said. She also talked about how neglectful he had been of his son.

Further, Sameera shed light on the social world of the gangster community. She spoke of how rivalries between gang members extended to their wives, about how Anis Ibrahim's and Chhota Shakeel's wives, like their husbands, never got along. She also narrated incidents after Salem broke away from Dawood and about how Anis barged into her house and threatened her. Sameera said she was scared of Salem and would have left him if she wasn't worried about the safety of her family members.

In a nutshell, Sameera described Salem as a cowardly person, extremely frightened of Dawood and whose only desire in life was 'fame, fame, fame'. Following is the verbatim transcript excerpted from the long interview:

Sheela: Tell me, is there any person who does not have a heart or a mind?

Sameera: When someone loves himself, he cannot love anyone else in this world.

Sheela: You have such guts that you spoke to Dawood one day. You were able to talk to Shakeel?

Sameera: Because I have nothing to hide.

Sheela: What is left with you that can be robbed?

Sameera: Prestige. I still have my honour.

Sheela: If you talk to someone, how will you lose your honour?

Sameera: You know, I am still living in a society with my son. If someone points fingers, saying that is her ex-husband, it would matter to me.

Sheela: So, you feel that this holds some meaning in America?

Sameera: In your society, where you are living among Indians, it does. They need something to gossip about.

Sheela: I wanted to ask one thing right from the start, what did Abu Salem want in his life, did you figure out?

Sameera: Name, name, name, fame, fame, fame.

Sheela: But this is fame in obverse?

Sameera: Look, he didn't understand what famous means and what infamous means.

Sheela: So, he wished someone would write 'don' Abu Salem?

Sameera: I think so, yes. I just asked him one day, you know, there are so many stage shows and how people come, big, big stars come up and they perform and people are so happy seeing these things, you know when they are entertaining someone and they clap their hands, they want to see them, meet them, love them, hug them, take pictures of them. [To Salem] Do you think that there is anybody who wants to do this with you?

Sheela: So, did he like the fact that people were scared of him?

Sameera: I don't know, but he didn't want to hear about it. He told me that 'people know me and respect me'. I told him that 'you know they don't love you or respect you. No one loves you or respects you. They are just scared of you because they love their families or the people in their lives a lot' . . . If there was an option for me to get out, I would have, long ago. But I could not tell this on his face.

Sheela: When the blasts happened and there was talk of you being sent away to this place or the other, did you see Abu Salem scared?

Sameera: He is a very scared person . . . He was in constant touch with me till my son was born. Till then, I was living in that place and he would come every night. I knew that if he did not come one night, he would surely come in the morning and sleep, eat and drink.

Sheela: Did he bring any star to your house?

Sameera: One or two had come. He asked me, would you come and I will introduce you to him.

Sheela: Who **** or **** or ****'? [names deleted]

Sameera: Please, I didn't tell you.

Sheela: But I have heard that he and **** decided to have their son's name common? [name deleted]

Sameera: He didn't even bother to tell this.

(From the conversation that follows, it seems Salem calls his son 'Papa'.)

Sheela: Did he ever hug his son?

Sameera: He was just two years old when he went away. You know, when he says he could get kids from Monica and he could do this and he could do that . . . He is just a child. He can live his life, let me live.

The way he talked never made me feel that he ever even thought of putting his son at a point where you would say that he loves someone.

Sheela: He had some priorities in life. He wanted to be someone?

Sameera: He was not a family person. I never lived a life that I would say was a 'married' life which means husband and wife sit together. We had never ever even eaten together. It was just about serving him and his life; sometimes he did not even want to see my face. I used to send his food with the servant. So people think I lived with him for fifteen years, but I didn't live with him even a single minute or not even a married minute.

Sheela: Didn't he ever tell you 'I love you' or 'Abu loves you', not even after he forcibly married you?

Sameera: No, he told me he wouldn't have married if he didn't love, as if saying that 'I' did something big for 'you'. He said my eyes were on you and I married you and gave you a good house and car and clothes. Everything was always like 'I' have this right on 'you'. He made me feel that even in front of a thousand people, I gave you this, I gave you food, I gave you drinks. I am into lots of *sher–shairi* recently.

Sheela: Yes, say?

Sameera: It's like . . . the world's at one's feet and the feet are in chains, you know, I always portrayed myself like that.

Sheela: So, you had to face fourteen years of exile?

Sameera: I always felt that I had food, but I was not hungry because it killed me . . . I had clothes, but I never wore good clothes and everyone in Dubai knows that I was always simple. I never wore jewellery on my body.

Sheela: When he used to go to Dubai, one or two visits to Anis's place took place. At that time, seeing him in that environment, what did you feel? Did he have a really powerful position?

Sameera: See, the things you are telling me about . . . I never went into that . . . environment where I could see him with others.

Sheela: No, but one is able to make sense of things?

Sameera: But when I was with the women, the women always had the priority that amongst all of us, Dawood's wife, Anis's wife, 'we are somebody' [that they were somebody] and 'you women, your husbands work under us'; so when they work under them, 'you work under us' and that I could never take . . . sorry . . . I never had buttered them . . . when I had my son's birthday, it was my son's first birthday . . . I wanted to do it very nicely . . . He didn't even bother to come to his son's birthday. I didn't even want him to. I had only my set of people who knew me as my son's mother . . . there was not a single underworld person there.

Sheela: Did anyone threaten you after the separation from Dawood?

Sameera: I never had the time to even talk to them.

Sheela: When the phone came or when men were sent to your home, was there any threatening?

Sameera: They knew that I was there, but they knew indirectly. When Anis called up and he was indirectly interrogating me—'where is your husband'—and all [that] bullshit because he [Salem] had this office and thus had his picture there. He asked for that picture and . . . tore it in anger. What they did was they sent all these people to my house, [saying] that they want the picture. Along with him, two of his brothers were also there, and all I told him was that you have come to take his picture, eight men to collect his photo, [for] just that bit of a photo eight men came. [They asked,] 'Where was Abu Salem?' I was very blunt, I said 'Do you tell your wife where you go? How do you expect me to know where he is?'

Sheela: Mustaqim?

Sameera: Mustaqim, Moin, Riyaz and five other people . . . three–four people, they came in cars full of people.

Sheela: So, they all came to you and looked for the photo . . . Why did you say that Dawood was better?

Sameera: Because I was very mad and I think at that period of time . . . (Chhota) Shakeel's wife had some . . . I think she had a birthday party or something. Something that she wanted to call me for. She called me. Shakeel's wife and Anis's wife never got along well . . . they both fight among themselves.

Sheela: Power play among wives?

Sameera: In my lifetime I would write a story on all the wives, how they lived . . . so she wanted to call me, she knew I never went much to many places but it was *niyaaz* (religious function) or something, so she forced me, that I would definitely have to go . . . she called me up and said all these things and I was mad at that point of time. So she said, 'Okay . . . I'll talk to him . . . This is not the way to behave.' And then I got a call from Shakeel: 'What happened?' I said, 'I have never been a party to any of your things, you know me, how

I am, the way I have lived . . . Have I ever interfered with your life or anybody's life or even been there to butter or do something wrong? Or harm someone? I have nothing to do with all of this. I always stayed away from all of this, so . . . I don't want anyone to come to my house because it is killing me from within myself . . .' Then Dawood called up. He said, 'What happened?' He assured me that 'after this nobody will be at you . . .' And he asked me: 'What happened, what did he say?' I said, 'This is the way he talked with me . . . and I don't agree to it.'

Sheela: Did you ask Dawood?

Sammmra: I told him directly: 'Do you ever tell them (your wives), did you ever do these things to them? He said no. I said, 'You should understand the way he talks to me, it kills me. Why not a different way (of talking), you know. Why do women come between your lines [conversation]? When men are there . . . why do you want to get any woman dragged into any of your things?' And he respected that. He said, 'I will make sure that nobody calls you . . .' and after that no one ever did.

Sheela: That was the first and last time that you had a direct talk with him or did you talk to him directly earlier as well?

Sameera: No, this was the first time I talked to him, and after that, they (Dawood and Salem) again patched up. I don't know how they patched up and then again they called it off . . . They patched up because Dawood had come to Dubai, I guess.

Sheela: So, again he called?

Sameera: He didn't call me any time.

Sheela: You talked to him just once?

Sameera: Ya, ya, on the phone I just talked to him once . . . then he is very . . . if I compare with any other people . . . he had that respect . . . at least talking nicely on the phone and I told him, 'See, whoever you are and I know you are Bhai, but I don't respect you for what you are. As a human being just because you are older to me, I respect you, but if this is the way you behave, if this is the way your brother (Anis) behaves, do you think I would have any respect for him . . . Every man is there for their own action and they are respected due to their own action.' Shakeel and Anis never got along with each other, never. No, I always see tension between the two women . . .

Sheela: Well, there used to be tension between their wives because the husbands did not get along?

Sameera: That's what they told me, both of them.

Sheela: Well . . . meaning Shakeel's wife would tell you?

Sameera: I have done so much for him, and what does she think of herself? That whoever's man he was, she was everything. She did not even know how to talk. I taught her how to talk properly.

Sheela: But tell me, what would you do at the parties?

Sameera: Nothing, I used to sit at one place and leave in half an hour.

Sheela: Did Abu ever tell you how to behave, how to talk at those parties?

Sameera: Oh yes. 'Don't be that rude and blunt.' 'You don't know how to talk to people.'

Sheela: Yes?

Sameera: He was too much into it. I never pushed him to let me go to any parties and he never pushed me. I always made excuses.

Sheela: So, you want to say that after your forced marriage, the married life you enjoyed was no married life at all?

Sameera: No.

Sheela: Even after that, why did you go on for so long?

Sameera (laughing): I was stretching his soul.

Sheela: Did he hit you?

Sameera: I have many stitches here (points to her forehead).

Sheela: Hit you?

Sameera: He had beaten me up in Dubai so much. He wanted to kill me also.

Sheela: How? Did he hit you with his hand?

Sameera: It was at a stage where the doctor said that

'if you would have been brought late, you could have been dead'.

Sheela: That means you kept quiet because of physical abuse?

Sameera: I could say that they threatened my family. I have gone through a lot of physical abuse, even Monica has gone through a lot of abuse . . . perhaps what she saw in two years and two days, you multiply it by fifteen years to [get] what I saw.

Sheela: Did he abuse you after he was drunk?

Sameera: No, he never drank in front of me.

Sheela: Then why did he hit you'?

Sameera: Because I used to . . . (affect) his soul.

Sheela: You used to argue with him?

Sameera: I was not arguing. I used to always tell him the truth. [I used to tell him] 'What would you get? Exactly what would you get by doing this to me?'

Sheela: And?

Sameera: I always came to conclusions that he was somewhere psychic or psycho.

Sheela: But you left for Dubai and later came to America?

Sameera: He used to hit me here as well.

Sheela: But you could have called for the police here?

Sameera: You don't understand. He had that power over me. My family is right there in India . . . I can't do even the smallest thing until and unless he is behind bars. And I know if he comes out, I'd be the first one that he wants to kill.

Sheela: Oh God! You think that?

Sameera: It's not the question of thinking, I somehow know it.

TWENTY-EIGHT

MONICA THE TURNCOAT

'I AM SINGLE AND UNMARRIED,' MONICA told Judge C.V. Subramanyam at the Hyderabad court. Her statement shocked everyone. Salem, not least of all.

Clearly, Monica had made a firm decision to break away from Salem. At some point of time during their incarceration in Lisbon, the realization had apparently dawned on her that she did not have to always be Salem's moll. She was only in her thirties and had her entire life ahead of her. She had spent the last six years in notoriety and ignominy—the first three of them running from the law, hiding from the law enforcers, taking refuge behind fake identities and then another three years behind bars. Humiliation and taunts were her constant companions from Lisbon to India. In prison, she had tried to delude herself at first, clinging on to Salem, crafting romantic and erotic letters. But it was not long before she saw the futility of it all. In her quest and desire for fame, she had landed herself in an abyss of infamy.

Soon after Salem and Monica landed in Mumbai, the mafia don was produced in the TADA court in Mumbai for his role in the serial blasts, while Monica was taken to Hyderabad by the CBI sleuths to investigate her involvement in the forged passport case. During the investigation, she denied procuring a fake passport in the name of Sana Kamil Malik, even though she was arrested in Lisbon using this identity. Her passport indicated that she had furnished her documents from Kurnool in Andhra Pradesh and had also signed on the papers personally. Monica was subsequently lodged at the women's prison in Chanchalguda Jail in Hyderabad.

Monica was remanded to judicial custody, but her imprisonment and the hearings in a Hyderabad court were not the end of her troubles. The Bhopal Police were keen on getting her too. After all, she was also accused of using a forged passport issued in Bhopal under the name of Fauzia Usman, while Salem used the identity of Danish Beg. The Bhopal Police wanted to begin interrogating her from the very day after her judicial custody in Hyderabad ended.

Monica spent those last months of 2005 and early 2006 shuttling between Bhopal and Hyderabad until she was convicted after a trial that lasted a relatively lightning-quick two and a half months. On 10 February 2006, Monica was sentenced to five years of imprisonment in the passport forgery case by the CBI special court in Hyderabad. She was shattered at the verdict, bursting into tears when it was pronounced.

During the course of the trial, Monica was allowed to attend proceedings in designer clothes and eat homemade food. But all these perks were quickly withdrawn as soon as she was convicted. She was given the choice of wearing a salwar kameez or a white saree and blue blouse. She chose the saree-and-blouse combination and received three sets, which she was expected to wash by herself. She was not Monica Bedi the starlet any more. She was now a prisoner, something she had never pretended to be in any of the twenty films that featured her.

The jail housed 330 prisoners and Monica was prisoner number 103. Since the jail was meant only for women prisoners, undertrials and convicts were housed in the same facility. Monica was shifted from the undertrial section to the barracks meant for convicts. Extremely depressed, she spent the first day crying in a corner of the barracks. As a convict, Monica was supposed to choose a trade in jail. She was expected to work in either the unit making incense sticks, candles and tooth powder or try her hand at stitching clothes through which she would earn Rs 10–15 daily, allowing her to buy some food from the canteen.

Monica might have laughed had she not been so crushed. A measly Rs 15 for eight long hours of hard labour? She was reminded of how she would leave tips to valets or waiters worth many multiples of the sum that was now her daily wage. She was used to earning lakhs of rupees from her film assignments and spending thousands of dollars on shopping trips in Europe. But there was now no option, and Monica, with some degree of forbearance, took on the role of a working prisoner. She began to work and mingle with the other prisoners. In the meantime, her lawyers assured her that they would appeal against the conviction.

It was about a month after her conviction that Monica Bedi's life took another turn, this time for the better. She was at work when she was told that she had a visitor. Tears rolled down her cheeks when she found out who it was. It had been four years since Dr Prem Bedi had met his daughter—the last time had been with Salem in Oslo. He had had to move an application and seek special permission from the court to meet her, but he had been successful. Monica recalled all those times her father had warned her against joining the film industry. She had stubbornly ignored those warnings. She apologized profusely. A dam had broken and she just could not stop. Needless to say, Dr Bedi forgave her.

The meeting lasted barely thirty minutes, but it infused a new hope in Monica.

When he walked out of the jail, Dr Bedi addressed the media. 'My daughter is innocent. I will do my best to get her acquitted,' he said.

Nothing drives humans more than hope and Monica was no exception. She grew more hopeful after her father's visit and began to look forward to life after her sentence. Every day was drudgery but Monica kept a brave front. She found out soon that her father had taken up her cause and had begun supporting her in the long appeal process; this bolstered her morale.

Soon after Dr Bedi's appeal against the verdict of the CBI court, things started looking up for Monica. The Andhra Pradesh High Court reduced her jail term from five years to three. Monica's father moved for bail in the CBI special court that had asked for her passport. When she said she had lost her passport in Lisbon, the bail was rejected. Subsequently, she approached the Supreme Court where she was granted bail. However, despite the apex court granting her bail in May 2006, her lawyers had to reckon with a pending case in Bhopal. This took another two months to sort out.

Eighteen months after being convicted—a whole five years since her arrest in Lisbon—Monica was released from jail on 4 July 2007. She emerged from prison accompanied by her father and lawyers. To her surprise, hundreds of people and scores of reporters and television crew had gathered outside the jail to catch a glimpse of her. The police had a tough time handling the swelling crowd. It was a stampede-like situation outside the Chanchalguda Jail.

The presence of crowds and the media left Monica stunned. A dozen microphones were thrust on her face. As she began to speak, those watching could see it was the ultimate aphrodisiac. She had wanted fame all her life and she knew she would be on national television networks all day. She spoke confidently, but kept her answers simple.

'I am very happy today. Finally, I have got justice. I am thankful to God. I will now spend some time with my family,' Monica said.

'I have learnt a big lesson,' she added. 'Earlier, I would trust everyone thinking that everybody is nice. Now I will be careful.'

The reporters and television crew surmised that this remark was meant for Abu Salem. What she said next was a major revelation to everyone. 'I am getting offers from Hindi and Telugu films. I am excited to come back to acting after a long time. I was missing acting in films. I plan to settle down in Hyderabad to act in Telugu films.'

There was thunderous applause and whistles from the crowd. The policemen, struggling to keep the jostling crowds at bay, were incredulous. For the men in uniform, she was an accomplice to one of the most notorious dons in India. The media had extensively reported on her efforts to evade the law for years. The courts had convicted her and she had served time in prison. Yet, the media was going crazy over her.

'I am sure this time I will make it. I will be careful in choosing films, producers and directors. I will only accept lead roles in films,' Monica said, perhaps implying that she would shun producers and directors with links to the underworld.

Finally, a reporter gathered courage and asked her how she had got involved with Abu Salem. This interrupted the flow of her speech. The smile on her face evaporated; Monica paused, gathered herself and said, 'It is over. I am looking forward to the future.' Her lawyers and family members hurriedly called off the impromptu press conference and got into the waiting cars.

Monica and her family left for Delhi to travel to her village Chabbewal in Punjab, where another rousing welcome awaited her.

TWENTY-NINE

SALEM'S SOJOURN TO SARAI MIR

THERE WERE TWENTY-FIVE ARMED MEN. THEY entered the general compartment and at once evicted all its occupants. Panic filled Bogie Number 1093 of the Mahanagari Express. Perhaps it was a train-jacking, the passengers thought to themselves. But their fears proved to be unfounded. The armed men were members of the Mumbai Police and probably belonged to the security detail of a VIP or possibly some local politician.

But they were wrong. The armed men in uniform were actually part of a security set-up for Abu Salem. On 11 October 2007, Salem was granted special permission to attend the funeral of his sixty-five-year-old mother, Jannatunissa, who had died of various illnesses two days earlier. Salem moved court on 10 October and was granted permission to leave the next day. Salem could make it only on 12 October.

In a hastily obtained order, the court gave him special permission to visit his ancestral village of Sarai Mir in Azamgarh. Since the Mahanagari Express was the first available train, the cops decided to take over almost half the general compartment and cordon it off with a rope to prevent any passenger from approaching their 'special cargo'. After this was done, the cops finally let the curious passengers occupy the other half of the compartment.

It was a calculated risk for the cops to escort Salem in the general compartment and they faced major flak from the media. Despite being accused of negligence, the police could not care less. The escort party was armed to its teeth, carrying carbines, rifles and guns. It was led by commandos and two senior officers of the Local Arms–II of the Mumbai Police. And they were quite used to last-minute travel arrangements and escorting high-risk individuals in long-distance trains. There had been very few untoward incidents reported, apart from the killing of Arun Gawli's aide Tanya Koli on the Vidarbha Express by gunmen from a rival gang.

As the train pulled in at the Varanasi station, the police did not use the common exit route on the platform, but asked Salem to alight from the opposite side, on the tracks. Since the platform was going to be far too congested and moving around in the crowd would have been risky, the isolated train tracks seemed to be a safer option. Salem got off the train twenty minutes after the other passengers, and the police led him into a waiting armoured van.

As Salem walked out, he saw a sea of people jostling with one another, waiting to catch a glimpse of the don. Clad in a casual white shirt, jeans and a cap, Salem enjoyed the attention he was receiving. In fact, he almost felt like a film star. He looked directly into the television cameras and smiled for them without shying away for even a moment. There wasn't a trace of shame or remorse in his eyes. He climbed into the government-issued Tata armoured van—with its reinforced doors—and then looked sheepishly out from behind the grilles. It looked like one of Mumbai's most powerful gangsters had been caged, defanged and declawed.

This made for great television and was repeated over and over for the next few days across news channels. After a little while, the vehicle drove off as part of a convoy of eight cars; with police personnel riding on bikes on either side of the van. The security detail would have given any politician a complex, particularly if they had been told it wasn't a VIP, but a gangster who was being accorded this treatment on the ninety-six-kilometre road to the sleepy village of Sarai Mir.

Sarai Mir is well known in Islamic educational circles because of its clutch of madrasas. The region had nurtured a rather communal mindset. The residents of this underdeveloped village, many of whom lived below the poverty line, were staunch Muslims who were slowly being radicalized. And thanks to Salem, Sarai Mir was now even more infamous. But the crowd took pride in this reputation and even felt good about being known because of Salem's shenanigans.

The crowd at Sarai Mir that waited for the gangster was overwhelming. An estimated ten thousand people had gathered that afternoon. It was the holy month of Ramzan. The Hilal Committee (the organization that reports on the sighting of the moon and declares Eid) had announced Eid to be two days later. The day Salem returned to his village was Jummatul Wida (the last Friday of Ramzan, which has special significance for Muslims), but instead of spending time in spiritual pursuits, the devout Muslims had begun converging in the Pathan Tola area where Salem had built a palatial house across his comparatively spartan ancestral home.

It seemed more like the funeral of a spiritual leader than that of the mother of a gangster. Salem himself was amazed at the crowds and saw this as a mark of his popularity. He raised his right hand and waved gently as he stepped out of the police van. The crowd erupted. The police guided him through the ruckus and brought him to the Baitul Uloom (the abode of knowledge) madrasa, where he was going to conduct his mother's last rites. Almost everyone who had followed him to the spot joined in to observe the *namaz-e-janaza*—the last ceremonial namaz performed for the dead before burial.

At the conclusion of the final prayers, Salem, along with three others, carried the bier on his shoulders and walked towards the dusty graveyard. The Barodi kabrastan was three kilometres away from their house and it took them over an hour to get there on foot. All the while, twenty-five policemen guarded him and the others simply followed. As he emerged from the graveyard after the burial of his mother, a television reporter accosted him and asked him to say '*do lafz*' (two words) on his mother's death. '*Maa toh maa hoti hai*,' Salem said solemnly into the microphone as he looked into the camera. After a brief pause, he continued, '*Do lafzon mein bayaan nahin kiya ja sakta*.' (A mother is a mother and her loss cannot be described in two words.)

After the burial, Salem returned to his home. It was a large white mansion, one of the most handsome buildings in the vicinity, surrounded by a barren playground, short trees, several raw-brick buildings and shaky housing societies. Salem walked up to his terrace, surrounded by cops and his own cronies. Clad in a green T-shirt, he leaned against the railing in the balcony and waved to the sea of people who had gathered below. People in the neighbouring buildings stood at their balconies to watch a man who was famous for all the wrong reasons. Salem smiled confidently, as his entire entourage surrounded him on the balcony. He put a foot on the railing to raise himself and then waved again like a film star.

'*Salaam alaikum*,' Salam said loudly.

'*Walaikum salaam*,' the collective reply reverberated.

Salem had begun using his newfound stardom to the hilt. As he was taken to his various court hearings across India—in the general compartment of the train like he had been to Azamgarh—people would approach him for his autograph. Ironically, Salem's biggest fan base comprised youths in their twenties. Salem flashed them his big smile, shook hands with them and signed autographs for them. In some cases, when his admirers did not have a piece of paper, they offered him currency notes—of Rs 100, Rs 50, Rs 10—for him to sign on. Salem would happily sign on them and declare generously, 'Preserve the note with my signature. When I am released from jail, I will give you back hundred times the value of the note bearing my signature.'

After this, it became a common sight at the Chhatrapati Shivaji Terminus or Bandra Terminus, the starting point for his journeys or even at Vashi Hospital where he went for routine medical check-ups. Everyone wanted Salem's initials on an Indian currency note. These train journeys and mass admiration became Salem's drug of choice to escape his jail travails. Laid low by the abandonment by Monica and the death of his mother, he now began to revive, reimagining himself as an Indian superstar.

THIRTY

SALEM'S ONE-WOMAN ARMY

ADVOCATE SHAHID AZMI WAS ONE OF the most controversial lawyers in Mumbai's legal circles. As a teenager, Shahid had crossed the border and received terror training in Pakistan and was subsequently charged under TADA. However, he was later acquitted by the Supreme Court. During his incarceration, he studied law and resolved to defend only those who were wrongly accused of terror charges. In a brief legal practice that lasted seven years, Shahid managed to get seventeen acquittals.

Like Salem, Shahid was also from Azamgarh. The don had heard of the lawyer's resounding victories and wanted him to defend him. Shahid refused. Around that time, advocate Saba Qureshi joined Shahid as a partner in his firm. Saba was barely twenty-eight years old, but her astuteness belied her age. She found that Shahid charged barely Rs 5000 for the terror cases which would take him months or years of hard work to turn around. Saba convinced him to charge a higher amount, and her influence eventually resulted in the lifelong train commuter buying himself a car. Saba also advised him to organize his legal work and take on cases other than defending those accused of terrorism. Shahid was impressed and smitten by Saba and proposed marriage. She readily agreed.

Their marriage was only a few months away when fate scripted Shahid's and Saba's story differently. On 11 February 2010, while Shahid was at his office in Taximen's Colony in Kurla, a suburb along the eastern spine of Mumbai, four assailants led by Devendra Jagtap barged in and shot him dead. Criminal lawyers had been killed in the past, but they usually had a suspicious record and dealings with the underworld. Shahid was a clean lawyer with no connection with them.

The Mumbai Police arrested the four assailants, including Jagtap, and claimed that they belonged to the Bharat Nepali gang. It was alleged that Shahid's killing might have been the Indian government's way of silencing a detractor since he managed to defend the terror-accused and get them acquittals, causing deep embarrassment to the state. His murder is still a mystery.

Years later, director Hansal Mehta made a movie on his life by the title *Shahid* with actor Rajkumar Rao playing the slain advocate's character.

Shahid's death drew the attention of the media and legal fraternity towards his reclusive partner, Saba. Her career was strong as well. She managed to get two Indians accused of conspiracy in the 26/11 attacks acquitted and provided logistical support to Ajmal Kasab and other terrorists. This not only earned her accolades, but got her noticed in legal circles.

One of Saba's clients was a man named Amit who was accused in a murder and kidnapping case. Amit delayed paying Saba's legal fee, finally telling her that Salem would pay on his behalf. Saba remained reluctant to ask Salem for money and began to contemplate quitting the profession altogether. Shahid's death had made her lose interest in legal work. Salem sent her message after message and she kept ignoring them. Finally, when she couldn't ignore the deluge of messages any more, she decided to meet him.

Saba was known to be impertinent, fiery, blunt and often a very outspoken lawyer. In fact, she had even misbehaved with some of the judges in their chambers, earning their wrath. This had made her quite unpopular in the fraternity, but her work and professionalism was such that no one could point a finger at her. Salem could not believe that this woman dared to talk to him in such a brusque manner. During their conversation, Salem learnt that Saba had been Shahid's partner and senior to Shahid. He immediately warmed up to her and offered her his brief. Saba was initially disinterested, but rose to the challenge when Salem asked, 'Are you scared to take my brief because you are a woman?' Saba had to prove him wrong.

'I may be a woman and not as experienced as the others, but I can turn your case around as none of your earlier lawyers did,' Saba retorted. Salem also boasted to her that had Shahid agreed to defend him, no gangster would have dared to kill him. But Salem was wrong. Within a few years of Shahid's killing, the same shooter Jagtap assaulted Salem in the high-security prison at Taloja.

Lawyers were making a beeline to represent Salem, knowing they would be in the limelight for defending such a high-profile client. However, Salem was not keen on hiring them; he was looking for top-notch lawyers such as Nitin Pradhan, who had represented over a hundred accused in the Mumbai serial blasts, and Majeed Memon, who later became a Rajya Sabha member. Sudeep Pasbola, regarded as one of the most proficient criminal lawyers in the city, was also among his battery of legal eagles.

Saba was the youngest and the least experienced of the lot. She was also perhaps the only one who was not in awe of Salem. Salem began to trust her almost blindly and delegated a lot of important work to her, including having her represent him in the Portuguese courts. Soon, she managed to notice major anomalies and discrepancies in the case. Saba managed to convince the Portuguese court through local counsels that the Indian government had violated the assurance it had given of prosecuting Salem only for the nine named cases; she sought that the Indian government stick to the charges approved by the Portuguese court.

For instance, one of the major accusations against Salem in the serial blasts case was that of delivering weapons to Sanjay Dutt. The Lisbon authorities had approved of charging him only under the Arms Act and for illegal possession of weapons. But the CBI also charged him with conspiracy in the blasts case which would attract the death penalty. Saba managed to change the game for Salem and turn the tables in his favour.

On 14 September 2011, the Tribunal Da Relação de Lisboa, the Portugal High Court, declared, 'In view of what has been stated above, judges of the third bench of this high court consider that the Indian Union while accusing and judging Abu Salem Qayyum Ansari for the fact described in points 3 to 8 of the new accusation framed under the case RC-1/93 CBI STF Mumbai violated the principle of specialty as it is understood in the Portuguese legal system, reason for which it considers these acts as illegal and decided to terminate authorization granted for extradition of Abu Salem Qayyum Ansari.'

The verdict threw the Indian government and the prosecution into a tizzy. Saba moved an application on 26 September 2011 in the courts saying that since the Portugal courts had terminated the extradition, Salem would no longer go to court. This infuriated the courts and the government. They were not willing to kowtow to the Portugal High Court and its diktat. Salem then demanded, on Saba's advice, to be shifted to the Portuguese consulate until the matter was resolved between the two governments.

The Indian government moved the Portugal Supreme Court challenging the High Court order. In its appeal before the Portuguese Supreme Court, the Indian government argued that the interpretation of the Portuguese High Court of the trial in various courts of the country was not correct and assured Portugal that the fresh charges levelled against Salem attracted a lesser jail term than the offences for which he had been extradited.

The Indian government made a dual appeal. One appeal was made on behalf of the Republic of India and its right to prosecute its accused, while the other was made by the public prosecutor. However, when a three-judge Supreme Court bench in Portugal presided over the matter, they first rejected the petition of the Indian government and its claims to privilege and rights of a sovereign nation. The government was asked to channel its pleas through a public prosecutor.

While hearing the plea of the prosecutor, the Supreme Court felt that the Indian government had indeed violated its executive promise and breached the terms of extradition. The three-judge bench unanimously agreed and upheld the termination of extradition. Two of them also sought that Salem be sent back immediately. However, the third judge said that there was no provision in the law to recall an extradited accused. Since there was no such precedent of violation and the Indian government was the first such violator of extraditions terms, the recall of Salem would be pursued through diplomatic channels.

The Supreme Court of Portugal passed its verdict on 11 January 2012. This came as a major shot in the arm for Salem and his defence team. But the Indian government refused to bow down to Portuguese hegemony. They immediately approached the Constitutional Court and appealed on the grounds that the Indian government, as a sovereign entity, had the privilege and prerogative to try its accused as per the norms and customs of the country's judicial system. The termination of extradition would therefore actually undermine the prerogative of the government. However, in its verdict on 5 July

2012, the Constitutional Court, which is actually on par with the Supreme Court of Portugal, conformed with the orders of all the earlier courts. This put the Indian government in a further fix.

Saba has already planned her next move to stay ahead of the Indian government and has moved to approach the European Union. This will not only make the task of judging Salem much more complicated for the agencies, but it will also heap more embarrassment on the government. Meanwhile, Salem's increasing trust in his young lady lawyer had got gossipmongers working overtime. Still mourning for Shahid, Saba began to get agitated at the wild allegations and rumours. 'Salem is only a client, please don't associate any other relationship to this,' she screamed in open court one day to a senior counsel.

THIRTY-ONE

SURVIVING REPRISALS

THE SHRILL SIREN SENT THE GUARDS at the Mumbai Central Prison into a panic and they ran towards the high-security barrack number 10. Two men were jostling on the ground and were separated amid much shouting and flinging of expletives. Salem was bleeding from his nose, chin, neck and arms. Mustafa Dossa stood there smugly, a bloodstained aluminium spoon in his hand. Nobody knows exactly how the scuffle began, but from the sharpened spoon, it was obvious that it was a pre-planned attack.

Salem was kept in barrack number 10 after a brief confinement in the Anda Cell. Over the five years, Salem had grown comfortable in his cell and had begun to see it as home. He had managed to get in some gym equipment, his designer clothes, stack of files, and some luxury essentials. He had also managed to get Italian marble fitted on the floor. Former associates and acquaintances had themselves shifted to the barracks around his, making his life that much more comfortable. His driver Mehndi Hassan, and Javed Siddiqui were housed close to him.

Two men from the navy, Manish Thakur and Emile Jerome Mathew, were also lodged in barrack number 10. Thakur was accused of killing his girlfriend Kausambi Layek in an Andheri hotel in 2005 and was subsequently lodged in Salem's barrack in 2007. Jerome had killed television executive Neeraj Grover when he found the latter at the house of his girlfriend, starlet Maria Susairaj. Jerome suspected Maria of infidelity and chopped Neeraj's body into a reported 300 pieces. In a gruesome aside to that tale, Jerome and Maria had sex twice in the same room, next to Neeraj's corpse lying on the floor. The couple then burnt Neeraj's body parts in the jungles off Manor.

Thakur was a naval engineer, while Jerome was a navy officer, a sub-lieutenant. Both these well-educated men became Salem's assistants of sorts in the jail. They helped him draft his legal pleas, fill out application forms, strategize on defence matters and understand convoluted legal documents. In fact, Thakur and Jerome became integral parts of Salem's think tank. Needless to say, they shared his meals and other luxuries in jail. Salem's clout and affluence made their lives easier in jail.

Over time, the gangster gradually decided to make further use of their skills and asked them to write his life's story. It thus came to be that a school dropout had two educated navy officers working as scribes for him. The autobiography projected Salem as something of a hero. Over hundred pages were handwritten by Thakur and Jerome in legible English on sheets of paper. Salem intended to pass on his story to a film director and demand that it be turned into a motion picture. He was certain that his story had the makings of a box office hit. All in all, Salem was lording over barrack number 10, treating it as his fiefdom. He was the uncrowned king of his barracks.

Mustafa Dossa, alias Majnun (so called for his womanizing), was another heavyweight in Arthur Road Jail. Charged with involvement in the Mumbai serial blasts and deported from Dubai in 2003, Dossa was regarded as the undisputed boss of the jail long before Salem entered the picture. Several gang members paid obeisance to him and rallied around him to enjoy the perks he had managed to procure either through court permissions or by greasing the palms of jail officials.

Once, on the occasion of Eid, Dossa obtained court permission to have *sheer khurma* (a Persian delicacy) in jail. The courts allowed him to have the delicacy, but the jail officials could not interpret whether the order was just meant for Dossa or it extended to all other Muslim prisoners. They decided to play safe and so Dossa threw a sheer khurma feast for the entire jail. This made him rather popular.

Over time, Salem and Dossa were happy to rule the roost in their own demarcated territories and neither came in the other's way. But their comfortable and luxurious prison life was shattered by a totally unrelated incident. Ajmal Amir Kasab, the lone surviving Pakistani gunman among the ten terrorists who attacked the city on 26 November 2008, was arrested by the police and, after a brief spell in police custody, was shifted to Arthur Road Prison. His security was assigned to the Indo-Tibetan Border Police (ITBP). Kasab's incarceration had converted the whole jail into a fortress even from the inside. Several accused and detenues were moved and reshuffled from their cells and barracks for security reasons.

Dossa ended up being shifted to barrack 10, regarded as Salem's stronghold. Dossa did not think much of Salem, having seen him play a small-time lackey in the Anis Ibrahim gang. Dossa's wealth and supporters ensured that he had the upper hand in this territorial battle, while Salem who was facing an acute cash crunch felt slighted by Dossa's attitude while staying in his fiefdom. The atmosphere grew tense with the two megalomaniacs trying to assert themselves.

Finally, on 24 June 2010, Dossa decided to teach Salem a lesson. The spoons were sharpened and Dossa decided to disfigure him knowing that Salem was extremely vain. He had figured right. Narcissistic to the core, Dossa's attack on his face left Salem totally rattled. The attack led Salem to be immediately shifted to Taloja Jail, while Dossa was transferred to Thane Central Prison. The government, too, was shaken by the attack. Any serious outcome would have left them red-faced in front of the international community. In fact, they had a tough time explaining the incident to the Portuguese tribunal.

Wasting no time, the minister of state for home, Ramesh Bagwe, decided to visit the prison and inspect the scene of the crime. Bagwe was shocked at the conditions in the jail. Addressing media persons, he said that the jail was like a five-star hotel where underworld members could get any facility for a price. Salem's cell had a bed, utensils and even semi-nude photographs of models, while Dossa's cell had huge tiffin boxes and a massive supply of fruit that could last several people two weeks. These two prisoners from the underworld were living very well indeed.

As a norm, the state government always sends the Dawood gang's rivals to Taloja prison to avoid showdowns in Arthur Road Jail with their arch-enemies. But these punishment transfers were soon converted into an advantage by gangsters who virtually ran their activities from behind bars. Arthur Road Jail, for example, is close to Dawood's stronghold in the Muslim segment of South Mumbai; so, it's easy for the gangster's couriers to pass on his messages to the prisoners. Taloja Jail is close to Dawood's rival Chhota Rajan's stronghold, Navi Mumbai. Rajan's trusted aide D.K. Rao was sent there instead of Arthur Road Jail after his arrest. Dawood's arch-enemy Arun Gawli too has been lodged in Taloja since his conviction in the killing of Shiv Sena corporator Kamlakar Jamsandekar.

The idea behind the construction of Taloja Jail on the outskirts of Mumbai was to decongest Arthur Road Jail, which is bursting at the seams with over 2100 prisoners, more than three times its designated capacity of 800 prisoners. Taloja Jail is still under construction and is expected to accommodate 2500 prisoners when it is completed and fully functional. Currently, it has 867 inmates, including Somali pirates, Bangladeshi migrants, members of the Indian Mujahideen and the Students Islamic Movement of India (SIMI) as well as eight accused in the September 2007 Malegaon blast case, including Lieutenant Colonel Prasad Shrikant Purohit. It also houses members of the Bharat Nepali, Ashwin Naik and Salem gangs. Salem and Gawli are the two dons lodged in the jail.

Taloja Jail, too, has its high-security anda-shaped

cellular structure, a double-storeyed one at that. Each floor has fifty cells of 10 feet × 5 feet. Salem inhabits one of these and is kept in solitary confinement. Thirteen cells next to his are vacant, so he has virtually no neighbour. Also, having suffered a violent skirmish in Arthur Road Jail, Salem decided to be discreet in Taloja. He knew that the only powerful man in the jail was a Dawood detractor, Arun Gawli, who had shifted there a year earlier in 2009. So, Salem decided to befriend him. Grapevine has it that the two occasionally chat in the open spaces within the 20-foot-high walls of Taloja. Salem soon regained his lost bluster and began threatening jail officials. He once reportedly threatened a jail staffer: '*Goli yahaan khayega ya bahar khayega?*' (Do you want to be shot inside or outside the prison?) It was this arrogance and Salem's growing unpopularity that paved the way for a near-fatal attack on him.

On 23 June 2013, Devendra Jagtap, alias JD, a sharpshooter of the Bharat Nepali faction of the Chhota Rajan gang, had returned late after his court appearance in Mumbai. It was around 8.30 p.m.; while his escort team left to unlock his cabin, JD strolled towards Vishwanath Shetty (Anna), another Rajan aide, whose cell was close to Salem's. JD engaged Anna in conversation for a while. Then he stealthily moved towards Salem's cell and saw the don was reading a newspaper. JD had concealed a countrymade revolver in his clothes. He whipped out the gun and fired at Salem. Salem, whose back was towards the door, was startled by the sound and the bullet whizzing past his face. He turned immediately and saw JD, who fired another shot. The bullet hit Salem's hand. He ran towards the corner where the bathroom is located when JD pulled the trigger a third time. But the bullet got stuck in the trajectory and he could fire no more. By then, Salem had also raised an alarm.

The prison guards, who had by now taken a good twenty minutes to unlock JD's cabin, came running to take him to his cell. Salem was badly shaken. Had JD aimed better, a single bullet could have spelled doom for him. Several questions remained unanswered in the incident. Who gave the gun to JD? Why was he not frisked at the entrance? How and why was he allowed to stroll towards Salem's cabin unhindered? Why was he not stopped by his escort team? Why did the escort party take twenty minutes to unlock his cell? The attack reeked of a full-fledged conspiracy. The government suspended four jail officials for their lax approach. Incidentally, JD is the man who killed advocate Shahid Azmi in 2010.

The Kharghar Police launched an investigation into the case and grilled JD. The sharpshooter confessed that he was given a supari by Dawood's right-hand man Chhota Shakeel. JD said he had spoken to Shakeel from inside Taloja Jail using two mobile phones. Shakeel had promised JD that if he managed to kill Salem, he would be made the leader of the gang in the jail. The gun was procured through one of JD's aides lodged in the same jail.

Salem thus survived a second attempt on his life by his arch-rival. The first one had been in New Jersey. The attack in Arthur Road Jail was more of a salvo fired at his ego and vanity than his life. But the attack in Taloja was a serious one. Shakeel had been after Salem ever since 2001 when he was in New Jersey, but Salem had managed to escape. Salem was left wondering how long his good fortune would survive.

Once again, advocate Saba Qureshi came to the rescue. She realized that the two attacks on Salem were blessings in disguise and decided to rake up an old petition his previous lawyers had filed in the European Court of Human Rights (ECHR), appealing to stall Salem's extradition to India. This was after the Portuguese government and courts had green-lit his extradition. The ECHR intervened and stalled the extradition, thus delaying it for a month or so. The ECHR is an international court established by the European Convention on Human Rights. It allows for applications against states that violate one or more human rights statutes concerning civil or political rights. The appeal can be made by an individual or a group or a state and the ECHR is empowered to deliver judgments or give advisory opinions.

Saba, along with her Portuguese counterpart, advocate Manuel Luis Ferreira, is drafting a plan to approach the Portuguese court and the ECHR to raise appeals on Salem's mistreatment in jail, the two near-fatal attacks on him, and the Indian government's failure to abide by the terms of extradition as ruled by the Portuguese Supreme Court.

If the ECHR takes note of the appeal and is convinced by the case presented by Saba and Ferreira, this can spell colossal trouble for the Indian government. Since the Indian government is not part of the European Union, the ECHR order will not be binding on it; but it will be mandatory for Portugal to obey the ECHR's dictates. The Portuguese government which is doing billions of dollars of business with India did not want to upset New Delhi for one criminal. So it was not seeking Salem's recall so aggressively. However, if the ECHR issues a clear diktat, then the Portugal government will have to pressure India to send Salem back. The Indian government may not have a say in such an eventuality and it might be forced to send Salem back, much against its wishes.

Will the don win this round? Only time will tell.

EPILOGUE

A DON-IN-WAITING

2 p.m., 26 May 2014, Mumbai Sessions Court

IT HAS BEEN ALMOST SIX MONTHS since I last met Abu Salem in court and tried to convince him to tell me his story. Salem is wearing a yellow shirt, brown trousers and black designer shoes today. Once again, I find him hungrily attacking his food. He has become leaner since I met him, but what really surprises me is his changed hairdo. He sports a much closer crop than his stylish haircut of the past.

An overweight but dangerous-looking officer attempts to block my way at first, but eventually allows me access. After a brief exchange of pleasantries, I come directly to the point. 'So when can we start discussing your story?'

'No, I don't want to waste my time on the book. I want you to do the movie script. It's the most amazing story and people will love to see it on the screen rather than read some book,' he tries to dissuade me again.

'I assure you that the book can be converted into a movie script and perhaps could even turn into a major film,' I persist, knowing the futility of trying to convince someone so stubborn.

'You are trying to reduce a Salman Khan to a Hemant Birje,' he shoots back.

I am taken aback by the analogy. Salman Khan has been responsible for hit after hit, while Birje was a one-movie wonder and a less-than-remarkable actor.

'I don't agree with your comparison, but it all depends on the potential of the story,' I try to reason with him.

'I know my life story is good. The audience will be hooked,' Salem says, wolfing down his food.

'Okay,' I concede, 'let's work on both the book and the movie script.'

'*Haan*, let me think about it and discuss it with my wife,' he says, matter-of-factly.

'Wife? Which one? You have already divorced Sameera, Monica is no longer in your life. Are you referring to the woman you married on the train?'

Mumbai Mirror has recently reported that Salem married a young girl from Mumbra, on board a train while he was on his way to Lucknow. The girl is at least twenty years younger than Salem and appears to have been brought in to troubleshoot for him. Salem is going through an acute financial crisis and has no one to look after his money which is locked in properties in Mumbai, Mira Road and his village, Sarai Mir. This girl, who was cheerily posting Salem's picture on her Facebook profile, is now apparently also controlling some vital decisions of his life. He begins to fumble. '*Jo bhi ho*, I want to ask my life partner and don't want to decide before asking her,' he says, cheeks reddening.

'When will you tell me?' I ask.

'Give me a month or a month and a half. By then, even some of my court cases will be wrapped up and I will be a relieved man,' says Salem, polishing off the last crumbs.

'What will you do once you are released from jail?'

'I will enter politics and fight elections,' he says confidently.

'How are you so sure of making it in politics?'

'I know I will win comfortably from my village. The seat belongs to me if I want,' the don in him is making an appearance.

'Which party will it be? Samajwadi Party?' I ask.

'No!' he says incredulously. 'Why Samajwadi Party?

I can even contest on a Shiv Sena ticket and win.'

The portly police officer indicates that I have taken up plenty of time and should probably leave. I promise to meet Salem again in a few weeks after he consults his 'wife'. I quickly take my leave.

I have decided to have a word with Monica Bedi too. After all, she seems to have turned a new leaf and has begun giving interviews to film magazines. She is evasive initially and pretends to not know me. Then she changes tack and stops responding to my messages. I recall my last meeting with her around five years ago in a suburban coffee shop. I was carrying out research for the present book as well as for *Mafia Queens of Mumbai* with a colleague.

It was early 2009. Monica was late by over forty-five minutes, but was apologetic. Very unlike a celebrity.

'I am extremely sorry for the delay,' she said, sitting down opposite us with her publicist joining her on the couch. 'This show is so competitive . . . I have been practising with my choreographer all day, so I just got caught up. Sorry again,' she added.

Monica Bedi was doing well for herself in life and had managed to start her career afresh. The show she was referring to was the third season of *Jhalak Dikhla Jaa*, which was going to hit the screens in the second week of April 2009. Monica seemed very nervous about the dance show. 'Cut-throat competition,' she put it succinctly.

Monica was dressed in a green T-shirt and blue jeans that showed off her slim figure. Her wavy hair streaked with golden brown was let loose and she barely had any make-up on her face, except for a tiny bit of gloss on her lips. A few people threw knowing glances at her, but Monica seemed indifferent as she made herself comfortable on the small cane couch.

The meeting had been fixed after a lot of unanswered calls and ignored messages. She did not want to meet me because she knew I was working on a book on Abu Salem and her love story. She had finally agreed to meet us over coffee at the JW Marriott Hotel in suburban Mumbai, following repeated requests to her publicist Shradha. The sole purpose of the meeting was to convince her to talk to us for the book. 'I am not so sure about this. The past few months have been so good and I have been so lucky that I don't want to rake up my past any more,' she said.

'But don't you want to clear the air?'

'I don't feel the need to. People have started accepting me despite my past. You've seen it on *Bigg Boss*,' she said, sipping her black coffee, referring to the successful reality television show which was her comeback vehicle. We noticed that she was deliberately avoiding the mention of Salem in our conversation. Despite her reluctance, we explained the premise of our book to her. Monica listened carefully and, for a moment, she seemed intrigued. 'Even if we do the project, how would I have to contribute?' she asked.

'Just a few sittings with us where you can tell us your real story.'

'Hmm . . . Do you know how many people have offered to do a film on my life? I've always refused.'

'Why?'

'I want to forget my past. It was traumatic,' she said.

'But your story is very interesting . . .'

'Yes, I know. Interesting for others, not for me, which is why I have got the copyright for my story,' she said.

'How can you have a copyright for your story when it is out in the media and heavily recorded in police dossiers?'

She didn't reply for a few seconds. Then she said, 'Uh . . . I will have to speak to my parents before I get back to you on this. They take all my decisions for me.'

We agreed, and then asked her about other issues, including her comeback on reality television shows, her alleged relationship with Rahul Mahajan and her recent decision to launch a religious music album. Though uncomfortable, she answered all our questions cautiously. When she had sipped the last of her coffee, she got up to leave. We shook hands, and she promised to get back to us in two days. The call never came. Neither were any of our calls to her ever answered. After waiting for years and pursuing her tirelessly, I decided to give up. She has done it again—avoided clearing the air on the Abu Salem story and her position in his life.

Her career has slowly progressed in the meantime. She won a cameo as a vamp in the serial produced by Sanjay Leela Bhansali, *Saraswati Chandra*, on Star Plus. She played a young stepmother to the main lead in the serial, but her story arc did not last long and she did not enjoy much screen time. Unable to get a foothold in Hindi movies, she tried her luck in films in other languages. She got a role in the Tamil film *Devadasi,* and in a Punjabi film *Sirphire* as the main female lead opposite Priyanshu Chatterjee. The movie was released in August 2012 and even won her an award for best debut. Suddenly, her fortunes started looking up and she got a role as woman cop in the Punjabi movie *Rambo Ranjha*.

The much-talked-about serial *Saraswati Chandra* was by now running successfully for two years, and the makers brought her track back in 2014. She is now the main antagonist.

She began giving extensive interviews to film magazines saying that her love for Abu Salem was pure and that she had been a victim of circumstances and didn't know who he was when she fell in love with him. She denied ever marrying him and consistently said she wanted to move on in life.

The Salem–Monica saga is one of the most intriguing mafia stories for the police, CBI, Bollywood, as well as journalists. It will always leave behind a plethora of unanswered questions. Salem apparently divorced Sameera or perhaps it was she who gave him an ex parte divorce. Monica now claims to have never married him and that it was only a brief association. But Salem has a nikahnama as evidence.

There is still a financial relationship between Salem and Monica. The CBI suspected that Salem legitimized his hawala earnings through investments in the US, the UK, and the Middle East. They claim that Salem's net worth is over $1 billion, approximately Rs 4000 crore, and that his legitimate wealth alone is pegged at Rs 1000 crore; Salem has kept Rs 200 crore for himself and his two ex-wives (if we consider Monica too as divorced, which Salem does not accept) jointly possess Rs 800 crore in cash and properties.

The remaining Rs 3000 crore is his unaccounted wealth or black money. The CBI came to this figure after calculating his transactions over a year's period—2000–01. While they still maintain that it is a conservative estimate and not an exact figure, they had taken into account various estimates and found that his account showed a balance of Rs 176,675 crore.

There is a strong suspicion that Salem's benaami but legal businesses in the Middle East are still managed by his close confidants in Dubai. The story of this master criminal and arch survivor is not yet over.

A NOTE ON SOURCES

This book, like most of my other books, has its roots in my career as a reporter. For nineteen years, during my stints as a crime reporter in various publications like the *Indian Express*, *Mid-Day*, *Mumbai Mirror*, *Asian Age* and as a stringer for *Time* magazine and *Rediff*, the mafia was everywhere. Over that period, I had strung together career graphs of members of the mafia, with first-hand telephonic interviews with the bad boys themselves, their not-so obliging relatives, extremely wary gang sympathizers and overzealous underworld informers, as well as personal interactions with investigating officers, prosecution and defence attorneys. When it came to the mafia, I made it a point to attend all the press conferences and police briefings.

A NOTE ON SOURCES

Abu Salem Abdul Qayyum Ansari of Sarai Mir of Azamgarh was part of my network of mafia contacts. Even after he snuck out of Mumbai and found refuge in Dubai, where all the Mumbai mafia had homed in on, he would agree for telephonic interviews. When he fell out with Chhota Shakeel and had to leave Dubai, he was still accessible for interviews.

I had already written about Salem's victims such as Pradeep Jain, Gulshan Kumar and Ajit Deewani, as well as his failed attacks on film-makers Subhash Ghai, Rajiv Rai, Rakesh Roshan, Aamir Khan, J.P. Dutta and others.

I have stacks of newspaper clippings, court documents, charge sheets, approver's statements, confessional statements, statements given to judicial magistrates under Section 164 of the Code of Criminal Procedure, and recorded interviews of witnesses. When Salem went off the radar of Indian agencies, it was difficult to keep track of him. My good friends at the CBI who had so generously helped me during my research on *Black Friday* stood by me again.

It was through them that I got access to copies of Salem's multiple passports with various assumed identities and those of his first wife Sameera's and Monica Bedi's—believed to be his second wife. I have his *nikahnama* in Urdu and its notarized English translation from the Karachi courts and clergy, indicating the solemnization of the Muslim nikah, replete with details of *meher* (alimony), names of qazis, witnesses, etc. I would like to believe they were married.

The fact was substantiated by Monica's love letters that were handwritten during her imprisonment at Lisbon jail. The letters are very explicit in nature and cannot be quoted. However, I would like to mention that the pair seemed to have great chemistry, and in the letters, Monica laments the fact that she could not be with her Babu (her nickname for Salem) on their second wedding anniversary.

I have various other court documents from the US Court of Gwyneth County, Atlanta, which reveal details of Salem's marriage with Sameera, his will for his only son Aamir, and the details of his properties in the US and other countries.

I also acquired documents from Lisbon courts, its High Court and the Portuguese Supreme Court that clearly indict Salem of several crimes, including that of perjury.

These documents were combined with massive tomes of legal papers and documents from Indian courts, including that of the specially designated TADA court, Bombay High Court, Supreme Court and the lower courts of Bhopal and Lucknow where he is being prosecuted for fake passport cases and fraud.

Most of the details have accurately been drawn from two basic reference dossiers of the Mumbai

A NOTE ON SOURCES

Crime Branch. The first one was called 'The Growth of Gangsterism' which was compiled by top officers of the Mumbai Police for in-depth orientation of their officers who did not have a perspective on the Mumbai underworld. The other was a detailed dossier, given to me by Deputy Commissioner Pradeep Sawant, which contains names and crime graphs of each and every gangster, and their gang affiliations and such other details. These two dossiers and files were also referred to and abstracts from them had been used in my earlier books, *Dongri to Dubai*, *Byculla to Bangkok* and *Mafia Queens of Mumbai*. So some of the nuggets of Salem's and Monica Bedi's lives were also picked from these earlier books of mine.

Several of Salem's friends spoke to me on the condition of anonymity. But I have recorded and transcribed those conversations as a backup, with the permission of my subjects. I have interviewed several film personalities, some of whom spoke to me in detail about Salem. These interviews have also been recorded. Several of Salem's relatives have also spoken to me and provided a lot of background on the family. I have, however, used my discretion and relied on the information given by them only to substantiate previous research.

Mumbai Police officers like retired assistant commissioner Iqbal Shaikh related the story of Salem's arrest by the Anti Terrorism Squad (ATS) at D.N. Nagar

A NOTE ON SOURCES

and how Salem was treated like a common criminal at the police station. It was Shaikh's foresight to fingerprint Salem and put him on the routine police records that would eventually save the day for the police in 2002. After the gangster was held in Lisbon in 2002, he denied being Salem and claimed vociferously that he was Arsalan Ali; however, his fingerprints told a different story. Among others, Pradeep Sharma who decimated Salem's gang in Mumbai, and Sachin Waze also helped me with a lot of information.

Ace Crime Branch officer and investigator Sachin Waze, who is a virtual gold mine when it comes to documents and authentic papers, was generous enough to share Salem's own handwritten autobiography with me. Salem had got this autobiography transcribed in English through his cellmates as he wanted a movie script to be developed from it. However, the Crime Branch managed to lay their hands on it and Waze shared it with me.

Several legal luminaries have spoken to me and shared a lot of information and insights in order to ensure that the account of various events in Salem's life remains authentic.

Last but not least, I dug into newspapers and reports filed by my highly esteemed colleagues in the profession. Chandramohan Puppala, my fellow crime journalist at the *Indian Express* and *Mid-Day* had scored several

A NOTE ON SOURCES

scoops on Salem. I have benefitted greatly from his stories. I have also relied on stories about Abu Salem by other Mumbai journalists.

To summarize, nothing that has been printed in this book can be called imaginary or fictitious. I have solid documentary evidence to substantiate the information, either through documents of the CBI, the Mumbai Police and the courts or through personal interviews duly recorded, or at the very least, through published news stories.